SOCIOLOGY *and* SOCIOLOGISTS

an introduction

EDITED BY LIAM KILMURRAY

Cover image © Shutterstock.com

Kendall Hunt
publishing company

www.kendallhunt.com
Send all inquiries to:
4050 Westmark Drive
Dubuque, IA 52004-1840

Copyright © 2023 by Kendall Hunt Publishing Company

ISBN: 979-8-7657-5730-7

All rights reserved. No part of this publication may be reproduced, stored in a retrieval system, or transmitted, in any form or by any means, electronic, mechanical, photocopying, recording, or otherwise, without the prior written permission of the copyright owner.

Published in the United States of America

Contents

1	**Introduction and Methods**	1
2	**Culture**	19
3	**Socialization and Culture**	27
4	**Social Interaction, Groups, and Formal Organizations**	43
5	**Social Stratification**	57
6	**Deviance**	71
7	**Family and Gender**	79
8	**Race and Ethnicity**	89
9	**Social Change and Social Movements**	101
10	**The State**	109

1 Introduction and Methods

Learning Objectives

1.1 Understand the sociology and the progress of the discipline through the years

1.2 Understand key figures and theoretical paradigms used within the discipline

1.3 Understand and be able to conduct scientific research

Sociological Imagination: The Ability to Connect

For those new to the discipline, you may ask, "what is sociology?" **Sociology** is a discipline that allows us to ask "why" of our surroundings. It allows us to answer the curious questions we have such as "why do individuals with higher amounts of education marry later than those who are not educated," "what is the relationship between religion and happiness," and "why do poor individuals have a significantly higher prevalence of health issues?" Sociology is the scientific study of human behavior and group interaction in society. It occurs every day, everywhere, and at various levels. Sociologists can study interactions at the micro- or macrolevel. It is a social science which concerns itself with understanding the relationship between humans and **social institutions**—established and organized systems of social behavior with an intended purpose—such as education, religion, health, or the media. You have probably already engaged in sociology and not even realized it. For example, have you been in a class and noticed that the teacher encourages some students, but perhaps doesn't encourage others in the same magnitude as the other students? This is an example that is founded in sociological concepts that will be explored later in this text. Sociologists study **social interactions**—behavior between

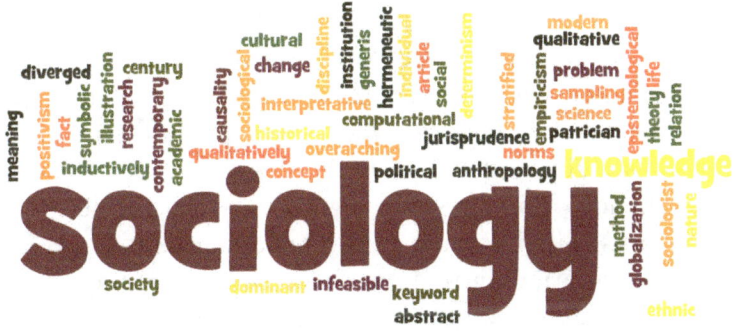
© Tang Yan Song/Shutterstock.com

Sociology: The scientific study of society, including patterns of social relationships, social interaction, and culture.

Social Institutions: These are established sets of norms and subsystems that support each society's survival.

Social Interactions: These are a system of behavioral and relationship patterns that are densely interwoven and enduring, and function across an entire society.

From *Exploring Sociology* by Mariah Jade Zimpfer. Copyright © 2018 by Kendall Hunt Publishing Company. Reprinted by permission.

two or more individuals with a specified meaning. These interactions help us to understand various mechanisms and how they function, or serve a dysfunction, in society.

What makes sociology such a fascinating and invaluable subject is that it allows us to understand not only the society within which we reside, but also allows us to see how we are connected to other societies around the world. Sociology helps us to understand our roles as social actors. On a daily basis, it is very easy for us to be myopic and only see our personal and individual problems. However, as social actors, we must understand that we are a part of a troupe on the stage of life and therefore, also, understand that the mechanisms which allow society to function—or as we will see throughout this text, dysfunction—are part of something larger. Social institutions which are found throughout society allow—or disallow—certain actions in society and therefore, result in a plethora of social phenomena. When we understand this relationship between our personal problems and larger social forces, we are using our sociological imagination. When we do this, we become sociologists who understand the social phenomena present in our society and world.

The purpose of sociology is to understand and generate new knowledge about interactions between humans and social institutions. Therefore, sociology is a social science, which suggests that it combines learned knowledge with the observation of society and how it is socially constructed to understand certain social phenomena. It employs the scientific method as a means to collect and analyze data regarding social phenomena. It is often criticized for being a "soft" science, distinguishing itself from the "hard" sciences—math, biological sciences, and engineering—because it specializes in understanding the interactions between groups and various institutions. Sociology can employ quantitative or qualitative methods—a concept we will explore further in this chapter. As social practitioners, sociologists recognize that while we study group interactions, we must also acknowledge the relationship an individual has with a group or a social institution. Agency is an important concept that allows us to understand the power dynamics of a situation and is often connected with structure. Power and the amount of agency an individual has is dependent on several variables. Agency is the ability of an individual; whereas, structure is best defined as patterned social arrangements. Everything in society is connected and therefore, those connections—or lack of connections—can significantly impact the mobility an individual has within society. For example, we can have agency in choosing the school system our child goes to. However, the structure of the economy system may prevent the opportunity to choose the school system because of financial and mobility issues. Therefore, it can best be summarized that while an individual can enact their agency, they may have constrained by structure.

Scientific Method: A systematic approach to researching questions and problems through objective and accurate observation, collection, and analysis of data.

Quantitative Research: Formal, objective, systematic process in which numerical data are used to obtain information about the world.

Qualitative Research: Primarily exploratory research used to gain an understanding of underlying reasons, opinions, and motivations.

Agency: The capacity of individuals to act independently and to make their own free choices.

Power: The power to exercise one's will and make choices on an individual basis.

Structure: The distinctive, stable arrangement of institutions whereby human beings in a society interact and live together.

Mobility: Shifting from one social status to another, commonly to a status that is either higher or lower; and can refer to either economic or social status.

While sociology concentrates on studying human phenomena, we must remember that unlike its fellow social science discipline psychology, sociology concerns itself with understand group dynamics rather than personal ones. We first learn about the world and our surrounding through our personal experiences. However, we need to recognize that our personal experiences and troubles do not tell the full story of society, rather they tell parts of it. Therefore, we need to engage our sociological imagination, which allows us to move from private troubles to larger social forces. For example, we often focus on the relationship between student and teacher to gauge the success rate of our education system. However, by focusing microscopically, we fail to recognize that there are other larger social forces that may encourage or inhibit a student's success in the classroom. For C. Wright Mills, he saw the sociological imagination as an intersection where biographies and history meet.

Critical Thinking: Sociology as a Science and a Practice

To understand the world around us, we simply cannot solely engage the sociological imagination; it merely is a lens with which we begin to see the world, by using critical thinking skills, we then become social science practitioners contributing to the field and community. Critical thinking requires us to be both open-minded and discerning. It allows us to move from accepting anecdotes as facts—such as in common knowledge—to disseminating the truth from rumor. For example, when reading an article on Facebook, it might seem like acceptable information and you may see many of your Facebook friends posting and "liking" the article. However, critical thinking should make you pause and ask the questions: "who wrote the article," "where does the article come from," and "when was it published?" These are other similar questions used in sociology as well to determine the truth from the anecdotes found in examining social phenomenon. It is important to use critical thinking because we live in an age where information is so easily spread, tailored, and often distorted, that if not questioned, wrong information may easily be spread. Wade and Tarvis (1997) have outlined the six simple rules to follow when using critical thinking. The example of vaccinating children will be used to understand each step.

> **Critical Thinking:** Mode of thinking—about any subject, content, or problem—in which the thinker improves the quality of his or her thinking by skillfully analyzing, assessing, and reconstructing it.

1. Be willing to ask any question, no matter the difficulty. Since the creation of vaccines, people around the world have come to understand them as a useful measure to save people's lives; some might even consider them an artifact of modernity. However, in contemporary times, there are growing numbers of people who are claiming that vaccines might be harmful for their children. Despite your family's beliefs or your history with vaccines, you need to be able to ask if vaccines are safe.
2. Think clear and logically. The vaccine debate is often very emotive because of what children represent in any society. They represent kindness, love, hope, a new generation, and parents are usually exceptionally protective of their children. Therefore, it might be difficult for parents to think that something they have been doing to protect their children might be harming them. To think logically, we need to get at the root of why people are challenging the use of vaccinations.
3. Use evidence to back up your argument. To ascertain the credibility of vaccines, you need to look at the evidence and ensure that it is credible evidence, not just popular. Wikipedia is often used as a source of inquiry for students, and the bane of a teacher's existence because it is easy to manipulate. However, if you look at the sources cited when looking up "vaccines," you

might see that there are credible sources used to create the article such as ones from the Center for Disease Control (CDC) or medical articles that have been peer-reviewed. These pieces of evidence are credible, and will also lead you to more credible pieces of evidence.

4. Acknowledge assumptions—including your own. We are not blank canvases. We have experiences and commonalties with many individuals; however, they should not persuade us to follow the truth. Perhaps, you received vaccines as a child and have not had any of the complications that many are attributing to vaccines; this does not mean you don't continue your chain of inquiry. There are many factors which are different from when you had vaccines to now: the type of vaccines, the amount of vaccines, how vaccines are made, and so on. Therefore, you can't assume that because you didn't have difficulties with vaccines that none may exist.

5. Do not use anecdotal evidence. Mostly, everyone knows someone who knows another person that through a distorted story can claim that the unthinkable happened to them. While this makes for interesting stories around the dinner table, it does not provide the necessary evidence to make a proper scientific conclusion. One of the arguments for not vaccinating children is the link to autism. While a friend of a friend might claim that the child became autistic after receiving vaccinations we must ask, "is the child autistic because of the vaccines or do we know the child has autism because of advancement in research in diagnosis?"

6. Be willing to admit when you don't understand your results or are wrong. One of the wonderful aspects of social science research is that it is similar to putting together a puzzle. However, sometimes we find that when the puzzle is finished, the picture doesn't resemble the one on the box. This is ok and it's all a part of research. The information we find, the conclusions that are drawn, is the new knowledge we contribute to the academy. In doing this, we understand social phenomena just a bit better and we contribute to the body of knowledge which helps others think critically through other social issues.

Sociology Through the Years

Now that we have a basic understanding of what sociology is and what it does, let's discover the genesis of sociology through the years. The sociology that we draw from today has roots spread across four historical developments: The Scientific Revolution, the Enlightenment, the Industrial Revolution, and Urbanization.

The Scientific Revolution

Toward the end of the sixteenth century, scholars began to understand the world through the use of natural sciences. This same philosophy was applied to the social sciences. It was thought that the same methods used to understand the natural world could be used to understand the social world, thereby, helping people to improve their conditions of living. Auguste Comte coined his term "social physics," which later became known as sociology, during this time.

The Enlightenment

Following the Scientific Revolution is the Enlightenment. This is a time in which French philosophers such as Diderot (1719–1784), Montesquieu (1689–1755), and Voltaire (1694–1778) believed that humans could understand science and apply it to their situations. The Enlightenment moves one step further from the Scientific Revolution in that it starts to clearly define such notions as human rights, liberty, and equality—topics that sociologists still grapple with today. It is also during this time that Émile Durkheim (1858–1917) emerges and begins his studies. Essentially, the Enlightenment is a time in which many hope that a more fair and just society will be created.

The Industrial Revolution

The Industrial Revolution originated in England during the eighteenth century. It is a time when society began moving from primarily being agricultural and living on farms, to living in cities and working with machines. The Industrial Revolution seemed promising because it offered an opportunity to improve production rates thus generating quicker profits. However, this is the time when many sociologists start to see the decline of society. This is where we start to see the beginning of Karl Marx's teachings regarding class, exploitation of laborers, and a socioeconomic understanding of society. Karl Marx (1818–1883) claimed that we start to see an emergence of two distinct classes, the bourgeoisie—owners of production, and the proletariat—those exploited by the bourgeoisie. For Marx, the only way to eliminate this process of exploitation was to overthrow the bourgeoisie.

Bourgeoisie: The social class that came to own the means of production during modern industrialization and whose societal concerns are the value of property and the preservation of capital, to ensure the perpetuation of their economic supremacy in society.

Proletariat: The social class that does not have ownership of the means of production and whose only means of subsistence is to sell their labor power for a wage or salary.

Urbanization

Urbanization is the last stage of development, and where many modern sociologists find their position. Industrialization encouraged people to move from their farms into the city; but as the need for workers in factories became even more of a demand, many more people moved into the cities. With the creation of bigger cities came the creation of more social ills. Cities were often overcrowded, dirty, unsanitary, had higher crime rates, and overall living and working conditions were atrocious. Many sociologists like Durkheim saw the cities as a challenge to how people lived and understood themselves in society. He claimed that urban areas challenged people's norms and that eventually they would come to reside in a state of normlessness, known as anomie. Anomie causes anxiety because from a very young age, we are socialized to a specific set of norms

Norms: Social expectations that guide behavior.

Anomie: The lack of norms; normlessness.

as taught to use by our family. When people moved to the cities, norms were challenged by the heterogeneity, which people were now encountering.

Historical Figures in Sociology

Auguste Comte

Auguste Comte (1798–1857) is credited with being the founder of sociology, and is also credited with the creation of positivism. He was a French philosopher who lived during the French Revolution, and his experience at this time combined with his intellectual capacity spurred him to begin examining the society in which he resided. Before he coined the term sociology, he concentrated on understanding science and began creating laws and theories to better articulate the phenomena he was experiencing. Comte believed that the two components of what he would later term sociology are social statics and social dynamics. For him, this epitomized the symbiotic relationship between how society is governed and how it evolves. He is most recognized for creating the law of the three stages which examines the progression of society and essentially helps us to understand in contemporary conversations the movement from the concept of dynamic sociology to social theory. The three stages are theological, metaphysical, and positive (or positivistic). The theological stage understands the world and how it operates via gods and by unseen forces. The metaphysical stage moves more toward understanding through various essences and causes. Lastly, the positivistic stage is understood as being distinguished based on human knowledge—gathering information and analyzing it using data rather than superstition. The positivistic stage is where sociology is born. It is the stage where Comte comprehends for social change to occur, we must first gather data.

Social Statics: The order of society; it includes structural components (e.g., family, government, and economics) and the interaction between these components.

Social Dynamics: The study of social processes, especially social change.

Harriet Martineau

Harriet Martineau (1802–1876) was, until relatively recently, an unrecognized sociologist. However, because of the tremendous contributions Martineau had made in the social sciences, we would be remiss in not discussing her. Martineau was an English sociologist who rose to prominence by first translating Comte's works from French to English, making them accessible to a wide array of audiences. She developed early on a passion for marginalized groups on which many of her works concentrated. She came to America and was astounded at the presence of slavery, lack of women's rights,

inequality in marriage, the plethora of class issues, and much more. Based on what she witnessed, she concluded that America was morally stunted as long as social injustices such as these remained. These themes are prominent in her extensive publications which contemporary sociologists are utilizing.

Émile Durkheim

Émile Durkheim is best known for setting the guidelines of social science research. During his time, he was a very prolific author whose work ranged from understanding social disruption in *Suicide*, to writing about religion in his Aborigine studies, and providing new ideas such as social facts. For Durkheim, social facts were important for us to study because they challenge the agency that we as social actors have. Since social facts are elements that operate outside of an individual but can impact an individual, we further understand the relationship between agency and institution. Social facts compel you to act in a certain way, which indicates that they are tied to the socialization process; and therefore, are behind many of the issues that we study in contemporary sociology. We can't explain why we might prefer only men's football teams rather than coed teams.

Social Facts: These are values, cultural norms, and social structures that transcend the individual and can exercise social control.

Durkheim is also credited with the concept of social solidarity. This allows us to understand the dynamics in which groups are formed. For Durkheim, group dynamics rested on two types of social solidarity: organic and mechanical solidarity. Organic solidarity refers to people coming together based on heterogeneous parts thereby, indicating that each person has a set of characteristics that is different from the others and the rest of the group comes to need those types of characteristics and vice versa. Mechanical solidarity refers to homogenous characteristics, groups that share similar language, customs, and so on. Durkheim claimed that while organic solidarity is necessary in society, mechanical solidarity tends to show stronger bonds.

Karl Marx

Karl Marx, unlike Durkheim and Comte, believed that in order for society to change, it needed to experience a revolution. Marx lived during the industrialization period and saw firsthand the exploitation of the lower class by the elite. Many of his extensive writings indicate that the bourgeoisie would stay in power as long as the proletariat allowed them to be there, and as long as the bourgeoisie had a group to exploit. Therefore, Marx gives us the social conflict paradigm. This paradigm, just like his teachings, indicates that as long as there is an unequal amount of or access to resources, then there will inevitably be conflict. In fact, we can consider Marx as someone who saw in to the future because he cautioned that eventually the economy would be concentrated more in the hands of the few thereby, leading small business owners and those who are self-employed to lose their jobs. This is something that we see today with the creation of "big box" stores such as WalMart and with social movements that encourage individuals to fight against big corporations by "buying local."

Max Weber

Max Weber (1864–1920) was a German sociologist who concentrated on examining the notions of bureaucracy. For him, bureaucracies, when functioning appropriately, served society well. However, as he noted in many of his works, the likelihood of bureaucracies functioning appropriately did not happen easily. His examination of modern bureaucracies helped paved the way in understanding their intricacies—and also their faults. Furthering this, Weber was also very instrumental in creating theories explaining economic and social organizations. Weber believed in the power of bureaucracies but he was apprehensive in that they may remove creativity and therefore, people would become locked in an iron cage of rationality with irrational consequences (Chambliss 2018).

Robert Ezra Park

Toward the end of the nineteenth century, sociology departments started to become more available in universities across the United States. Most notable were the University of Kansas (1889), the University of Chicago (1892), and Atlanta University (1897). The most notable of these is the University of Chicago which gave way to being known as the Chicago school of sociology. Prominent figures such as Robert Ezra Park (1864–1944) created the study of urban sociology here. The Chicago school of sociology led the way in studying racial issues, class issues, the homeless, and plethora of social issues found in the urban areas of the United States. The sociologists at the Chicago school of sociology left their offices and headed to the streets to find out what was going on in society.

W. E. B. DuBois

W. E. B. DuBois (1868–1963) was an exceptional sociologist and civil rights leader. He lived during a time when "separate but equal" was the norm; but for him, the norm—just like many other sociologists at the time—was to challenge this notion. Many of his writings, such as the *Souls of Black Folk* (1903), condemned the hostility that allowed for racism to remain prevalent. He coined the term double-consciousness which meant that Black Americans were constantly aware of being both American and Black.

Robert K. Merton

The period following World War II saw a shift in sociology from qualitative models to quantitative analysis. Robert K. Merton (1910–2003) is also well known for his work on deviance (Merton 1938) and he created what is known as "middle range" theories. These theories rest between large grand theories such as those brought forth by Marx and Durkheim and quantitative studies. Lastly, Merton (1968) is also known for his concept of latent and manifest functions, concepts now common in sociology.

C. Wright Mills

C. Wright Mills (1916–1962) coined the term sociological imagination to illustrate how sociologists see the relationship between private issues and public problems. While many of the themes in this text are relatable, we must always remember to view them through the sociological imagination. This suggests that we view social phenomenon as social issues, rather than personal problems. As Mills' concept suggests, this enables its possessor to understand the larger context of the issue by first noticing the issue within himself. Sociologists view and understand the world through the interactions that individuals have with larger institutions. An example is the notion of white privilege. While an individual of Caucasian descent may claim that they don't feel as though they are privileged, we must recognize that this statement is through the lens of the individual, not the group. White privilege is the systematic oppression of other racial and ethnic groups vis-a-vis formal institutions—such as the legal system. Mills is also significant in that he believed that if knowledge was used appropriately, then society could improve. A concept that resonates with many sociologists.

Women in Sociology

It would be remiss to discuss the foundations of sociology without paying tribute to the women who helped make the discipline what it is. We are only recently fully unearthing the voluminous works by great female sociologists such as Charlotte Perkins Gillman, Mary Wollstonecraft, Aline Valette, and Jane Addams. Many women throughout the centuries have been involved with social issues, but have often been turned away due to the highly intensive patriarchal system in place. During their lifetimes, they were often dissuaded from being involved and despite many of them feverishly publishing, would not have been granted serious audiences. Today, we are recognizing what these women gave to the discipline and relish in the knowledge of society that they have produced.

Theoretical Paradigms

Theoretical paradigms, or sociological theories, are best understood as lenses which help us make sense of the social phenomena that we see. Theoretical paradigms are neither wholly right or wrong, but rather an interpretive perspective. The paradigms that we use in sociology are understood as examining

> **Sociological Theories (paradigms):** Are statements of how and why particular facts about the social world are related.

micro- or macrophenomena and therefore, a paradigm is either labeled as a microlevel paradigm or a macrolevel paradigm. The theoretical paradigms are structural functionalist—or also known as functionalist, symbolic interactionist, or conflict. Feminism, while not a social paradigm, falls under the umbrella in conflict as it details the relationship between uneven power distribution resulting in inequality between the sexes and gender. Symbolic interactionist is a microlevel paradigm because it concentrates on the reading of symbols, languages, media, images, and belief systems—to name a few—and how they are used to understand meaning and how people in society interpret those meanings. It examines small processes and it primarily concerns itself with understanding individual behavior based on these processes. These interpretations are always based on small-scale interactions; however, they are not based on small groups. For example, we can examine the institution of education using the symbolic interactionist perspective. A symbolic interactionist would examine how acts of labeling students can influence their approach to and success in school.

Structural functionalist and conflict are considered macrolevel paradigms because they concentrate on interpreting the relationships between members of society and large, multilevel and multivariate organizations or social structures that impact individuals in society. It concentrates on understanding how society is a stable organism and how various mechanisms maintain that stability—or instability. In sociology, it is just as important to look at what is not present, as is what is present. Structural functionalists will examine how other institutions, and mechanisms within those institutions, provide stability. For example, they will examine how the family unit provides stability in acculturating members to established norms, beliefs, and values in society.

The conflict paradigm primarily concerns itself with examining the imbalance of power relationships in society and how this prevents individuals with gaining economic and social mobility. When sociologists examine such issues as racism, sexism, classism, ageism, and so on, they often use the conflict paradigm because it is most suitable in understanding how power dynamics affect agency and therefore, result in the marginalization of groups based on specific characteristics. A sociologist who employs the conflict paradigm when examining issues of classism might indicate that classism exists because the elites—or the bourgeoisie—are exploiting the working class—or proletariat.

Theoretical Perspectives and Founding Theorist(s)	Structural Functionalism Émile Durkheim	Social Conflict Karl Marx	Symbolic Interactionism Max Weber, George Herbert Mead
Assumptions about self and society	Society is a system of interdependent, interrelated parts, like an organism, with groups and institutions contributing to the stability and equilibrium of the whole social system.	Society consists of conflicting interests, buy only some groups have the power and resources to realize their interests. Some groups benefit from the social order at the expense of other groups.	The self is a social creation; social interaction occurs by means of symbols such as words, gestures, and adornments; shared meanings are important to successful social interactions.
Key focus and questions	Macrosociology: What keeps society operating smoothly? What functions do different societal institutions and phenomena serve for society as a whole?	Macrosociology: What are the sources of conflict in society? Who benefits and who loses from the existing social order? How can inequalities be overcome?	Microsociology: How do individuals experience themselves, one another, and society as a whole? How do they interpret the meanings of particular social interactions?

Source: Chambliss and Eglitis (2018).

Designing and Conducting Social Research

As stated earlier in this chapter, the purpose of a sociologist is to understand and create new knowledge about the world around them. In order to create new knowledge, we must engage in sociological research. Sociology involves the scientific process in order to gather, analyze, and report data. Just like the social world is unique, so too, is social science research. We can either begin a project by engaging in **deductive reasoning** which suggests that we move from rather large and general ideas to using **inductive reasoning** which allows us to understand the problem at hand by first examining the data that are collected and letting it "speak" to us. We can also employ

Deductive Reasoning: Logical process in which a conclusion is based on the concordance of multiple premises that are generally assumed to be true.

Inductive Reasoning: A logical process in which multiple premises, all believed true or found true most of the time, are combined to obtain a specific conclusion.

a variety of research methods to gather data. Many of the popular methods for qualitative research are interviews, participant observation, and fieldwork. For quantitative methods, we employ such items as surveys. Quantitative research allows us to "quantify" information which then allows us to answer broad questions. For example, if you wanted to find out how many students in your class have car insurance and what company they buy their insurance from, you could take a survey. Qualitative research allows us to examine "qualities" or to add depth to the research. In order to qualify your survey, you could have a short answer question asking students "why they choose to buy their insurance from a specific company?" The best research projects employ both qualitative and quantitative methods, known as **mixed methods**. By employing mixed methods, we create a very nuanced report that provides very detailed information.

> **Mixed Methods:** The process that uses multiple ways, specifically research designs, to conduct research; it may also contain both qualitative and quantitative elements.

Employing the Scientific Method

When we gather research, we need to be careful. Data will always tell us something, but are we sure we understand what it's telling us. For example, suppose a study is conducted, which shows that pizza sales on a university campus are twice as high on Tuesday than they are on Wednesday. Based on this data, we could conclude that more people who attend Tuesday classes enjoy pizza. However, this might be misleading. When we do further research, we find that the reason pizza sales are twice as much on Tuesday as on Wednesday is a result of their being twice as many students attending classes on Tuesday than Wednesday we realize that there truly isn't an increase in sales, just an increase in the student body. When we realized that there was a third variable that impacted how we read the results, we realized that the increase in students on Tuesdays was the cause, we unearthed what is known as a **spurious relationship**. Earlier, we assumed that there was a direct correlation between students attending on Tuesday and pizza sales, this is an example of a **causal relationship**.

> **Spurious Relationship:** False correlation between two variables that is caused by a third variable.

> **Causal Relationship:** A relationship between two variables that show direct causation.

We also need to be cautious when we are conducting research because we need to be sure that our results are both **valid** and **reliable**. Validity means that we have data over what we said we were going to study. Valid results are results that accurately represent the concepts and measurements presented in the study. Reliability refers to replication of a study. For example, if a survey is administered, multiple times assessing the relationship between pizza sales and the student population at a university, the results that are produced over the several times that the survey is administered are the same or very similar. A study can be reliable, but not valid. Incorrect results can be reproduced; this is why it is essential that we operationally define our research question and analyze our data thoroughly.

> **Valid:** The degree to which an instrument, such as a survey question, measures what it is intended to measure.

> **Reliable:** The degree to which a measurement instrument gives the same results each time that it is used.

Sociological Research: Investigating the World

Defining the Research Question

As discussed earlier, we need to first frame our research question. The research process is reflexive. You may have a research question and use that to decide what methods you will employ, but may also revisit the question when you start to collect data. A research question is a work of art, it must be adjusted, critiqued, analyzed, and put under scrutiny for it to stand the test of social research. When we set out to engage in social science research, we must first organize our ideas and our approach. Sociologists often ask the question "why," but when we ask this question in our research, we need to be very specific in exactly what we are asking. For example, we can't ask "why are people overweight?" The question has piqued our curiosity but we need to take it a step further, we need to **operationally define** what we are asking. What kinds of people? Where are the people located that we are curious about? What age? What race? What gender? An appropriate research question tries to understand the relationship between two or more variables. "Why are people aged 25–40 who live in low socioeconomic neighborhoods significantly more obese than those aged 25–40 who live in high-socioeconomic neighborhoods?" is a more appropriate question. It tells us which demographics we are looking at, location of people, and what we are looking at—obesity.

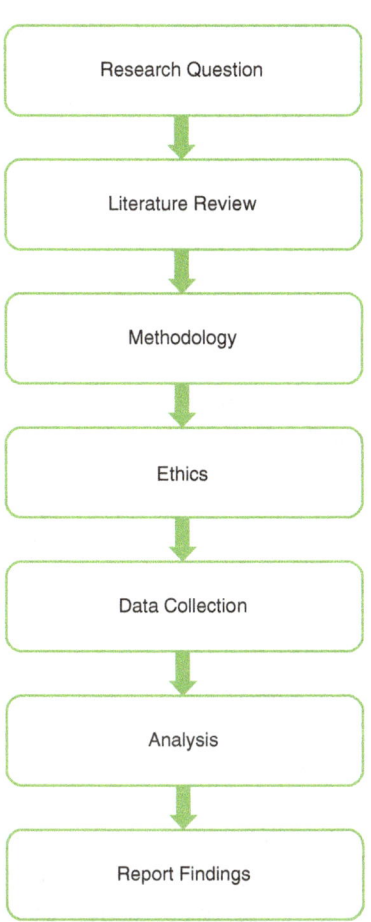

Operationalization: The transformation of an abstract, theoretical concept into something concrete, observable, and measurable in an empirical research project.

Literature Review

After deciding what the research question is, you need to review the existing literature to see what studies have been conducted involving the variables in your question, and what the results are. Literature reviews can be exceptionally helpful because they organize the research around your topic so that you quickly and adequately assess what methods have been used, what the popular and relevant conversations are about your topic, and most importantly as a researcher where you will input yourself in the literature. When reviewing the literature, you might also realize that it will help you to refine your research question.

Method Selection

After reviewing the literature, you should be able to assess what methods would be best for you to use. Is your project quantitative, qualitative, or are you employing a mixed method approach? These are questions that you will want to ask yourself when decided what methods to use to collect your data. We will now take a look at some of the popular methods that social science researchers employ survey, fieldwork, detached observation, participant observation, experimentation, use of existing information, and participatory research.

Survey

Surveys are usually associated with quantitative methods. They are an excellent method to use when you want to collect large amounts of information that you can quickly sift through, thereby, giving you a snapshot of the group being sampled. For example, if you want to assess how many students at the various levels in the university purchase textbooks from the university bookstore then you can send out a survey online asking questions such as "What level are you? Freshman, Sophomore, Junior, Senior," "Do you buy your textbooks from the university bookstore? Yes, No." Then you can quickly tally up the answers and come up with a conclusion. Surveys are also used, often, as a first step in deciding what other methods to employ. For example, if I am examining the relationship between textbook sales and students' income, I might realize that after sending the survey, that many students who are low-income groups do not buy textbooks from the university bookstore, but rather a third-party member. By understanding this, I might decide to conduct participant observation at the third-party locations.

No method is perfect. Surveys seem glamorous, but they are actually quite tedious and expensive to assemble. In order for a survey to produce valid data, you need to ensure that the questions are tailored to the audience who will be completing the survey. You also need to think about delivery methods for the survey, should it be paper-based or electronic? Surveys also tend to be expensive. It takes time and resources to craft the perfect survey, have someone—or a team—analyze the data, and also the resources with which to conduct the survey.

Fieldwork

Fieldwork, also known as ethnography, is a technique that is borrowed from anthropology. When you employ this qualitative method, you are "living with the tribe"; meaning, that you become a part of the community that you are studying. For example, when I conducted my research in the Appalachian region, I lived in Kentucky for 6 months. I went to the same grocery stores, restaurants, everywhere, that my participants went to. By doing this, I came to know firsthand what it was like to experience the issues I was examining. Fieldwork gives you an opportunity for your community to see and interact with you, but also for you to fully submerse yourself in the culture.

Fieldwork: Work done in the field to gain practical experience and knowledge through firsthand observation.

There are a few drawbacks to fieldwork. It can be expensive because you have to pay to travel and live with your community. Sometimes, it could be dangerous depending on several factors. For me, it had the potential of being dangerous because I was living in the mountains and during my study, there were several snowstorms that occurred. As a native Houstonian, I did not know how to drive on ice/snow or what precautions I needed to take in case I was snowed in. This is where my community members helped, because they told me what I needed to do. This brings me to my last point. When you engage in fieldwork, you want the members of the community to stop seeing you as a researcher and start seeing you as one of them—but with the ability and resources to share their stories. When this happens, the acceptance of the community members is a wonderful thing. However, caution needs to be taken in that you don't "go native," suggesting that you forget you are there for the purpose of research. When this happens, you run the risk of losing your objectivity.

Detached Observation

Sometimes our research investigates topics that might be dangerous such as drug or gang activities, to name a couple of examples. In order to research these topics, we can take an approach which allows us to gather data while ensuring our safety. **Detached observation** is when we observe individuals and their activities from a distance. We record notes, and then analyze them hoping to gain insight. For example, if I were studying where homeless individuals frequent, I might drive around or park on a corner and make observations of where homeless individuals choose to camp. Without approaching them, I can make some arguments as to why they choose their campsites in a specific manner, perhaps, because they are closer to food establishments, or they are covered, for example. By doing this, I ensure that I am safe; however, this doesn't produce adequate results. There is a lot of speculation and uncertainty around my results. Unless I interact with the homeless individuals, I won't truly know why they establish their campsites in certain locations rather than others. Therefore, detached observation allows us to record information about potentially dangerous individuals in society, but is not wholly useful because we can't get their side of the story.

> **Detached Observation:** A perspective that constrains the researcher from becoming in any way involved in the event he or she is observing.

Participant Observation

Participant observation is a useful method, particularly when engaging in fieldwork, because it allows you to participate in daily activities such as working with a local food bank, and recording your observations. It also allows for the opportunity to give back to the community by volunteering; and furthermore, it shows that you are committed and dedicated as a researcher. Participant observation allows you to get a true sense of the daily nuances of the community with which you are observing, more so than any other method. Unfortunately, because this is a qualitative method, it relies on interpretation of observations. It is very difficult to take notes and analyze them in the moment, or to take notes after the activity that you are participating at is completed.

> **Participant Observation:** Research technique characterized by the effort of an investigator to gain entrance into and social acceptance by a group so as better to attain a comprehensive understanding of the internal structure of the society.

Experimentation

Experimentation is sometimes used in social science research. We employ experimentation when we want to control for some variables and observe how other variables react. For example, perhaps, I want to study the relationship between amount of television watched and performance on tests for high school-aged students. My claim would be the more hours of television watched results in a lower grade on tests. My independent variable would be the amount of hours of television watched. My dependent variable would be the grade received. Similar to other methods, experimentation can be costly as you may have to create a particular environment.

> **Experimentation:** Measure the effect which an independent variable (the "cause") has on a dependent variable ("the effect").

Use of Existing Information

Sometimes when we try to address our research question, we come to realize that someone has already collected the data. There are thousands of data sets by reputable sources that offer both quantitative and qualitative information that can be used for analysis in your research question. By using existing information, it cuts down on cost, time, and bureaucratic practices such as approval from a review board. The drawback is that the data sets may not have all of the information that you need, and you may not be able to replicate the study if your research question asks something that is not located within the data set.

> **Existing Information:** Any kind of data that has already been gathered, such as newspaper articles or preexisting data sets, that can be used for research.

Participatory Research

Participatory research is research which allows community members to become involved in the research process alongside of you. When you enter into a community to conduct research, you don't want to leave as soon as the data has been collected. You want to teach community members the kinds of tools necessary to help them make the changes they wish to see in their community. Perhaps, I am studying the effects of nonprofit agencies in rural communities in the United States. It might be beneficial to engage community members in either joining current nonprofits or to help them start their own. This way, the work can be carried on well after you have left the community. By doing this, you give community members power and agency to place in motion the kinds of change they would like to see. While participatory research is very rewarding, it also comes with drawbacks. The project that you start with community members might not be the same one that they carry on. Furthermore, there can be power struggles between community members in deciding in how the project should carry on after you have left.

> **Participatory Research:** An approach to research in communities that emphasize participation and action.

Ethics

When we do research, we need to be concerned with two elements: ethics and objectivity. When you assume the role as a researcher, you need to ensure that you are operating by very strict codes of ethics. Your university, the institution which you are employed, and the discipline to which you are housed under, all have their own set of ethics that you must abide by. Social research often asks very personal, private questions in order to help us understand large social issues. Because of this, we need to take care that we are ensuring the mental and physical well-being of our participants. During the Nazi War Trials in Nuremberg, Germany, it was proclaimed that from that point forward anyone engaging in any type of research must abide by strict ethical codes so as to not repeat the atrocities that happened during World War II. The Nuremburg Trials, as they came to be known as, are used as an example when researchers embark on their data collecting journeys. Additionally, we need to be concerned with our objectivity when we conduct research. As stated earlier in this chapter, we are not blank canvases; we come to each situation with our own experiences and opinions. However, when we conduct research, we need to be as

> **Ethics:** Set of principles that guide social science research; emphasizes protecting subjects in research.

> **Objectivity:** Assumes that a truth or independent reality exists outside of any investigation or observation.

blank as possible so that we do not taint the information we are gathering. Often, when we conduct research, we are being observed as much—if not more—as our subjects. If we are not objective with our research, then we run the risk of misinterpreting or understanding our results. We could assume things about our study that need not be assumed and a plethora of other issues. The goal in research is to be objective as absolutely possible.

Significance of Sociology and Social Research

Sociology is present in every community around the world. By employing sociology, we allow ourselves to fully take part in the social diversity that is present in various communities. However, examining social diversity also brings with it its own set of challenges. We often look at other cultures through the lens of our own, known as ethnocentrism. It is difficult not to do these because we have been socialized to our community and culture's set of norms, values, and beliefs—as have other individuals. Therefore, we can use sociology to help us understand cultures and work in unity. By using our knowledge of the world around us, we can be active agents that participate in a multitude of social events around the world. When we engage our sociological imagination, we begin to see a larger, more nuanced picture of the world and our place within it. One way that we accomplish this is by being researchers, investigators of what we see and experience. By investigating scientifically, the world around us, we merge our experiences with others and begin to fully appreciate how colorful and vibrant it truly is.

Activity

Imagine that you have been given a grant of $30,000 by your university to spend on a research project. By using the themes and elements discussed in this chapter, complete the statements below:

Research Question: _____
_____
_____

Literature Review: _____
_____
_____

Methodology: _____
_____
_____

Data Collection: _____
_____
_____

Analysis: _____
_____
_____

Report: _____
_____
_____

2 Culture

What Is the Difference Between Society and Culture?

A **society**, on the broadest scale, is a group of people who share a culture and institutions that guide and represent their social interactions with each other. Although it can also be defined as a group of people gathered for a common cause, such as the "Religious Society of Friends," this chapter focuses on the broader notion of society. **Culture** is the general beliefs, values, norms, and behaviors that a group of people tend to adhere to. Although society and culture are terms that are often used synonymously, they are not exactly the same thing. Whereas a society is the people themselves, a culture is the things that dictate how those people interact and even communicate (e.g., their language, their religion, their art, their literature, their form of government).

Types of Societies

Many of the earliest sociologists believed in the "evolution" of human society. Most descriptions of societal evolution are illustrated with societal stages, where groups start as simple societies and then gradually change into more complex and organized societies. The type of society a group lives in will be a fundamental influence on their understanding of reality as well as their values and beliefs. Societies are often categorized into the following six groups (arranged from the simplest to the most complex):

- hunter-gatherer,
- pastoral,
- horticultural,
- agrarian,
- industrial, and
- postindustrial.

A **hunter-gatherer** society survives primarily by "living off of the land," or by hunting/fishing/gathering plants already present in the land within which they live. These societies tend to be nomadic unless resources in an area are abundant. Although no longer common, hunter-gatherer societies continue to exist. Examples include the Kalahari bushmen in Africa's Kalahari desert, the Sentinelese of India's Andaman Islands, and the Pirahã of the Maici River in Brazil (Czartoryski, 2011).

A **pastoral society** focuses on domesticating animals and using these animals for food. These societies are less nomadic than hunter-gatherer societies but can be if moving is a necessity to keep the animals fed. Current examples of pastoral societies include many of the Bedouin tribes of West Africa and the Arabian Peninsula (although some Bedouins have abandoned pastoralism), the Kochi of Afghanistan, and the Pokot of Kenya and Uganda (Seelinger, 2017).

A **horticultural society** relies on simple means to cultivate plants for food. These societies are often nomadic, depending on how abundant the environment is in plant growth. Current examples include the Yąnomamö tribe of the Amazon River basin, the Birom of the Congo River basin, and the Hanunóo of Mindoro Island in the Philippines (O'Neil, 2009).

Agrarian societies use technological advances such as irrigation, more advanced farming equipment (e.g., large, heavy plows), and often animal labor, to produce crops on a larger scale than horticultural societies. Establishing a profitable farm means being stationary and tending to a favorable piece of land to grow certain crops for longer periods of time. Crops are stored and used for consumption and bartering. In ancient and medieval times, agrarian societies included the most dominant, powerful civilizations on Earth, with examples including Ancient Egypt, Ancient Greece, Ancient Rome, Medieval England, and Medieval France. However, they are less common today.

Industrial societies rely on machinery to produce goods, including food production. Factories emerge and specialize in the production of specific goods. England, Italy, and Germany began to industrialize in the 1600s and 1700s, with mass industrialization in the United States occurring during the 1800s. Examples of leading industrial societies today include China and Mexico.

Postindustrial societies rely not only on technology and machinery for the production of goods, but also on the selling of services and knowledge. Individuals specialize in different vocations, many of which are associated with helping other people, such as doctors, professors, lawyers, and cooks. The United States, Germany, and Japan are examples of modern postindustrial societies.

Marx and Conflict Theory

Karl Marx (1978) emphasized how culture makes people who they are (as opposed to how the people make the culture). Marx proposed that all aspects of society, including both the personal characteristics of individuals within the society and the cultural elements used by that society, rest on the material or economic conditions that exist within that group of people. In Marx's words, "The sum total of these (material) relations of production constitutes the economic structure of society, the real foundation, on which rises a legal and political superstructure and to which correspond definite forms of social consciousness" (p. 4).

To illustrate this concept, Marx (1978) describes changes in peoples' sense of self-worth and purpose as a result of the shift of many nations from an agrarian society to a capitalistic industrial society. Before the rise of capitalism, people raised their own crops, built their own houses, provided for their own families, and developed a sense of self-worth and purpose from these activities. After capitalism, people began working for others to obtain a wage to buy things from other people. A person no longer produced everything he needed, but now worked for someone else with little to no control over what he produced, competing with others to obtain a better wage to buy what he needed. As a result, people experienced a diminished sense of self-worth and purpose.

The economic system dominant in most industrialized societies—capitalism—changed the culture, what individuals within the society valued, and the reality in which they lived. Taking this one step further, conflict theorists tend to view culture as an entity created and fueled by those in power (e.g., the owners of major industrial companies, and the politicians, law enforcers, and religious leaders who do their bidding) to control the rest of society (e.g., those who earn wages working for these major industrial companies). For example, the element of culture known as religion is viewed as a tool of the powerful to encourage exploited workers to accept their poor status in this world while focusing on obtaining a glorious afterlife.

Social scientists today (particularly conflict theorists) are careful not to categorize industrial societies as superior to nonindustrial societies. This is not because technology is a negative thing in itself, but rather because of the perception that it is often used by those who can afford it (the rich) as a way to exploit the less fortunate, as illustrated in Marx's (1978) depiction. Would changing the lives of those who lack the power of technology make it better or merely change their lives to something different but equally bad? While Marx believed that the shift from more "technologically primitive" agrarian society to more "technologically advanced" industrial society did not improve the situation of most working-class people, he also believed that capitalist societies, by means of social change and revolution, will eventually evolve into utopian societies where all citizens share all things equally.

Functionalism and Culture

Durkheim: Organic and Mechanical Solidarity

As opposed to the emphasis of conflict theorists on culture as a tool to protect the best interests of powerful industrial leaders in the capitalist system, structural functionalists *tend* more toward attempting to describe how the elements of culture known as "social structures" function to benefit society. Emile Durkheim, who held to the methodology (positivism) of Auguste Comte, sought to describe how societies change as they become more populated and industrialized (Durkheim, 1997). Based on his concept of **social solidarity**, which is unity based on interests, standards, and cultural objectives, Durkheim proposed that societies are held together by one of two types of social solidarity: mechanical or organic. **Mechanical solidarity** is found in simpler, traditional societies where family ties and smaller social networks are present. Mechanical solidarity is characterized by a low level of interdependence where individuals depend on their own family units to provide for all their needs. Moreover, these societies show a strong consensus concerning norms and values and there is a strong pressure toward conformity. As societies become more populated and industrialized, they change to organic solidarity. **Organic solidarity** is characterized by a high level of interdependence. Since the population of the society has increased and has become more dense, there is a greater need for a division of labor where individuals begin to specialize in certain professions. Individuals no longer depend on their family units for medical care or protection, but a doctor and a law enforcement officer. The division of labor emerges to better cater to the needs of the growing society and better utilize newfound technologies. But as the population increases, norms are not as resilient, and conformity is less of a demand. Both Emile Durkheim and Karl Marx conceived that as society become more industrial, that individuals would begin, or at least be at risk, to feel alienated. Unlike Marx who foresaw this alienation as a product of capitalistic oppression and greed, Durkheim believed alienation, or purposelessness, would arise in individuals as society grows in population and complexity. Norms become less resilient and social ties loose. Durkheim classified "the absences of social norms" as **anomie**, and normlessness, particularly a lack of norms tied to morality, would lead to purposelessness. Durkheim's theory is similar to Ferdinand Tonnies's concepts of *Gemeinschaft* and *Gesellschaft*. According to Tonnies ([1887] 1961), *Gemeinschaft* refers to a community with a small population comprising a small division of labor and informal social control. *Gesellschaft* is a larger society with a greater population and complex division of labor but with loose social bonds.

Parsons: AGIL

Functionalists such as Talcott Parsons described culture as an abstract guide that represents (for the most part) the desires of the people who live within a shared environment. "Cultural objects are symbolic elements of the cultural tradition, ideas or beliefs, expressive symbols or value patterns so far as they are treated as situational objects by ego and are not 'internalized' as constitutive elements of the structure of his personality" (Parsons, 1970, p. 2). Here we see that Parsons views culture as a distinct and separate entity from the individual (or groups), though he proposed that the cultural system interacts with individuals on different levels. Culture is more than the sum of the institutions that exist within a society, but instead shapes or defines the institutions. The culture sets the logical parameters or expectations for members of the group. However, people (groups) can determine how "the game goes" by their interaction with cultural parameters, and can even cause cultural changes. Functionalists stress that culture provides the information (or programming) so that social entities like institutions can instill (via socialization) into individuals the means necessary to survive (as a group), hence creating or maintaining stability and equilibrium. Parson's suggested that all societies, to some degree, must adhere to an understood societal template if those societies are to survive ("progress") and achieve equilibrium. He described this template using the acronym A-G-I-L. "A" refers to adaptability—all societies need to adapt to the environment and provide a means to distribute resources to the people, to "make a living." "G" refers to goal attainment—all societies must not only set goals but also obtain (or aim at obtaining) them ("Where are we going?" "What direction is our society headed?"). "I" refers to integration—all social entities and institutions of a society must be (to some degree) in accord or consistent (harmonious) with one another concerning society's goals and its parameters for providing for the people. "L" refers to latency or latent pattern maintenance—a society must be able to spread the aforementioned factors (A-G-I) to future generations. Holidays are a good example of latent pattern maintenance in action. U.S. society celebrates Martin Luther King day, Memorial day, and others because they represent values and goals of American society, and celebration of these days are passed on to upcoming generations (children get these days off from school).

Symbolic Interactionism

Symbolic interactionists analyze culture in a somewhat different manner from conflict theorists and structural functionalists. Structural functionalism and conflict theorists are concerned with large-scale changes in and influences on society (macroanalysis), whereas symbolic interactionism focuses on face-to-face interaction (microanalysis). Car emblems, the symbols of food and drink companies, religious insignias, team logos, and other similar symbolisms are topics of interest for symbolic interactionists. What one wears and what one drives, among other things, can communicate messages to different groups in society. Emojis express meanings via text messages. **Technoculture** is the interaction of culture and technology. Verbal (spoken and written) communications and nonverbal (hand gestures, facial expressions, and mannerisms) communications contain symbolisms that guide social interaction.

Language

From the works of Edward Sapir and Benjamin Lee Whorf arose the principle of linguistic relativity, also known as the Sapir–Whorf hypothesis.

> Human beings do not live in the objective world alone, nor alone in the world of social activity as ordinarily understood, but are very much at the mercy of the particular language which has become the medium of expression for their society. It is quite an illusion to imagine that one adjusts to reality essentially without the use of language and that language is merely an incidental means of solving specific problems of communication or reflection. The fact of the matter is that the 'real world' is to a large extent unconsciously built up on the language habits of the group. . . . We see and hear and otherwise experience very largely as we do because the language habits of our community predispose certain choices of interpretation. (Spier, pp.75–93)

Basically, an individual's understanding of reality and the things she perceives is determined, or at least influenced to a great degree, by how her language communicates those things. Neither Edward Sapir nor Benjamin Whorf specifically formulated a hypothesis called linguistic relativity theory or the Sapir–Whorf hypothesis. Social scientists combined the conclusions from the works of these linguists and created the linguistic relativity principle. Over time, many social scientists have found support for the basic concept of linguistic relativity. For example, some researchers have found that just as color and time terminology varies by culture, the terminology used also influences how color and time are perceived (Boroditsky and Gaby, 2010; Roberson, Davies, and Davidoff, 2000). Some feminist theories suggest that, for instance, the English language (and others) is biased in favor of the male in terms of both syntax and semantics and therefore shapes how women are viewed generally in society. Critics of this theory, and the linguistic relativity theory, suggest that it is difficult, if not impossible, to prove in an empirical manner that language semantics and syntax create perceptions.

Levels of Normalcy

Culture can be represented in both material and nonmaterial forms. **Material culture** is the physical objects and architecture that represents the beliefs and values of a particular group of people. Examples of material culture are certain types of foods, temples of worship, types of cars, and so on. **Nonmaterial** culture is the nonphysical things that represent the people. Values, beliefs, norms, language, and institutions are some of the examples of nonmaterial culture.

One form of nonmaterial culture, **norms**, can be described as the expectations that guide certain behaviors in specific settings. Norms can be broken down into three different categories: folkways, mores, and taboos. Norms serve as a means of social control, but are relative to the culture a person is in and also vary in relation to social setting and time. What was normal for a woman in the 1960s in the United States might be abnormal for a 21st-century American woman. Normal behavior at church might be different from normal behavior at school or in a prison. William Sumner stated, "Whenever a group has a group purpose that purpose produces group interests, and those interests overrule individual interests in the development of folkways" (Sumner, 1906, p. 81). The group controls the behavior of the individual through sanctions. **Sanctions** are the ways individual behavior is controlled by the group via punishments and rewards. Sanctions vary in degree. A positive sanction can range from a simple "thank you" or smile for holding open a door for someone to a monetary reward for being a concerned and caring neighbor. These things are rewards for being "normal." A violation of a social norm might lead to a negative sanction, which can range from a cross look from others around you to time in prison, depending on the perceived norm violation. You would be considered "abnormal" if you violate a social norm. Sanctions vary in degree because norms vary in degree.

Folkways, Mores, and Taboos

Folkways are expectations concerning behavior pertaining to casual social interaction, like covering your mouth if you yawn or standing in line at a store. You are expected to do these things by others, but violation of these norms typically does not bring heavy sanctions.

Mores are expectations concerning moral attitudes. Sumner made the following observation concerning mores, "When the elements of truth and right are developed into doctrines of welfare, the folkways are raised to another plane" (p. 64). Bullying is an example of a more in Western cultures. Hurting animals, voyeurism, and telling sexist jokes are other examples. The sanctions for these behaviors tend to be more severe than folkways in that there is a moral attitude that condemns them.

Taboos are expectations or prohibitions pertaining to behaviors that are considered extremely repulsive. Incest, cannibalism, and physically/sexually abusing infants are examples of taboos in most cultures. Taboos are more extreme than mores and often lead to laws enforced by the government prohibiting associated behaviors.

Psychopathy/sociopathy: Both psychopathy and sociopathy have traditionally been defined as antisocial personality disorders, according to the *Diagnostic Statistical Manual* (5th ed.; *DSM-5*;

American Psychiatric Association, 2013) used by psychiatrists to diagnose mental illness. Those affected with this disorder are deemed as having a "pervasive pattern of disregard for and violation for the rights of others." The *DSM-5* further illustrates that individuals subject to this diagnosis possess a "failure to conform to social norms with respect to lawful behaviors, as indicated by repeatedly performing acts that are grounds for arrest." Norm violation, in this sense, can lead to a diagnosis of mental illness.

Ethnocentrism and Cultural Relativity

The term ethnocentrism is often thought of as the belief that one's own group is superior to others. More accurately, **ethnocentrism** is the estimation and perception of other cultures based on one's own group standards. Sumner (1906) wrote, "For our present purpose the most important fact is that ethnocentrism leads a people to exaggerate and intensify everything in their own folkways which is peculiar and which differentiates them from others. It therefore strengthens the folkways" (p. 18). Ethnocentrism has the positive benefit of creating social solidarity in that it assures the people who employ it that their culture is better off than others. A negative consequence of ethnocentrism is prejudice that might lead to discrimination and oppression. **Cultural relativity** is the belief that norms and cultural practices are relative to the culture that exercise them. The phrase "to each his own" would be an appropriate way of expressing cultural relativity. Cultural relativity can benefit a group that has a diverse composition intending to create or maintain some form of social integration. However, cultural relativity can be dangerous when it leads to the relativist fallacy. The relativist fallacy is when all cultural practices are viewed as valid and acceptable. Some cultural practices may violate the human rights of others, such as female genital mutilation or genocide.

Social Movements

A **subculture** is a group of people that differs in some ways from the greater society, having some distinct norms and values (Mormons, Trekkies, bodybuilders, goths, bikers, etc.). **Countercultures** are groups of people whose norms and values differ extensively from those of mainstream society (radical feminists, various racial organizations, some animal rights groups, etc.). A countercultural movement can activate cultural or social change. **Social movements** are organizational structures (and their activities) that challenge mainstream culture and those deemed more powerful in light of a perceived oppression. A social movement's influence may be evaluated based on the amount or quality of social change that occurs accordingly. In observing social change, William Ogburn (1922) proposed the notion of cultural lag. **Cultural lag** is the notion that nonmaterial culture changes slower than material culture. Material culture, like technology, changes rapidly and at a larger scale than nonmaterial culture, which tends to resist change and remain fixed for a far longer period of time. This disparity between material and nonmaterial culture in relation to social change is often the precedent for social problems and the rise of social movements.

References

American Psychiatric Association. 2013. *Diagnostic and Statistical Manual of Mental Disorders.* 5th edition. Washington, DC: R R Donnelley.

Boroditsky, L., and A. Gaby. 2010. "Remembrances of Times East: Absolute Spatial Representations of Time in an Australian Aboriginal Community." *Psychological Science* 21 (11): 1635–39.

Czartoryski, A. May 27, 2011. Amazing Hunter-gatherer Societies Still in Existence. *Hunter Safety Blog: HunterCourse.com.* https://www.huntercourse.com/blog/2011/05/amazing-hunter-gatherer-societies-still-in-existence/

Durkheim, E. 1997. *The Division of Labour in Society.* Translated by W. D. Halls, intro. L. A. Coser. New York, NY: Free Press.

Marx, K. 1978. *The Marx-Engels Reader.* Edited by R. C. Tucker. New York, NY: W.W. Norton & Company.

O'Neil, D. 2009. Horticulture. *Patterns of Subsistence: Classification of Cultures Based on the Sources and Technologies of Acquiring Food and Other Necessities.* San Marcos, CA: Palomar College. https://www2.palomar.edu/anthro/subsistence/sub_4.htm

Ogburn, W. F. 1922. *Social Change with Respect to Culture and Original Nature.* New York, NY: B. W. Huebsch.

Parsons, T. 1970. *The Social System.* London: Routledge & Kegan Paul Ltd.

Roberson, D., I. Davies, and J. Davidoff. 2000. "Color Categories Are Not Universal: Replications and New Evidence from a Stone-Age Culture." *Journal of Experimental Psychology General*, 129 (3): 369–98.

Seelinger, L. July 12, 2017. 10 Nomadic Communities and Their Fascinating Lives. *The Culture Trip, Ltd.* https://theculturetrip.com/africa/articles/10-nomadic-communities-and-their-fascinating-lives/

Spier, L., A. I. Hallowell, and S. S. Newman. 1983. *Language, Culture, and Personality: Essays in Memory of Edward Sapir,* 75–93. Westport, CT: Greenwood Press.

Sumner, W. G. 1906. Ed. Keller, A. G. *Folkways: A Study of the Sociological Importance of Usages, Manners, Customs, Mores, and Morals.* Boston, MA: Ginn and Company.

Tonnies, F. 1887/1961. Gemeinschaft and Gesellschaft. In *Theories of Society.* Edited by T. Parsons, et al., 190–201. 3rd edition, Vol. 1. Glencoe, IL: Free Press.

3 Socialization and Culture

Learning Objectives

3.1 Understand the process of socialization

3.2 Learn the agents of socialization

3.3 Define concepts of norms, values, and beliefs

3.4 Explain the relationship between culture and class

Socialization: an Ongoing Process

Sociologists study the process of **socialization** and who we become, how we are influenced, and what kinds of social and economic access we have in our life. From the moment we are born until the day we die, we are constantly engaging in a process of socialization whether it is at home, school, with our peers, or even by watching television. The way we come to understand the world, and ourselves, is a constant process between us and the **agents of socialization**, which will be discussed later in this chapter. In this chapter, we will discuss the "nature versus nurture" debate and the stance that sociologists take. We will also examine the agents of socialization and various institutions, which impact our lives.

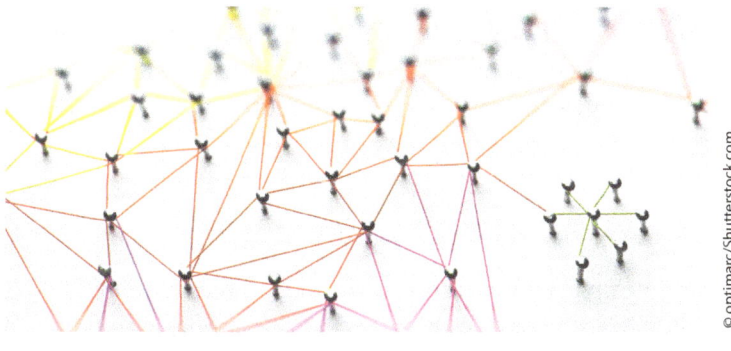

Socialization: The process of learning to behave in a way that is acceptable to society.

Agents of Socialization: Socially accepted institutions where socialization occurs.

The Social Self

As noted, socialization is an ongoing process in which we learn about ourselves and the society around us. Through the process of socialization, we learn how to construct our identity and understand how others think about roles that they have within their societies. Socialization is not only a process but also a way to think about how we are connected; it helps us to understand and produce culture. Even more significant is that it helps us to understand the norms, values, and beliefs in our society and others.

For many decades, researchers and social scientists (Coleman and Hong 2008; Ridgeway and Correll 2004) alike have debated between the relationship of nature versus nurture: the argument deciding if people behave the way they do because they are "born that way" or if it is because of the environment. As sociologists, we claim that there are certain aspects of an individual that are innate; but primarily, it is nurture that encourages—or discourages—an individual to behave in such a manner. Ultimately, nature may allow for opportunities, but nurture is what makes those opportunities possible. In order to explain this relationship, I draw on the example of language. Social scientists acknowledge that biology is responsible, for example, for how our bodies, such as our tongue or the structure of our mouths, is created by our genes. But, social scientists claim that it is not the structure alone which explains how we understand language. Our tongues and mouths do not teach us how to speak, to interpret the words and tones in a conversation, all of that is through the process of socialization, interaction.

Studies have indicated that socialization and human interaction are vital in order to allow individuals the opportunity to secure agency and autonomy for themselves in society. The most notorious case which illustrates this concept is the story of "Victor." Victor was a boy who was found by Jean-Marc-Gaspar Itard—a medical doctor in France—in the 1800s (Shattuck 1980). It is still not known how Victor came to be alone in the woods, but what was clear is that he lacked the ability to communicate and interact with humans as beset by the norms of the society at the time. Victor was taken in by Itard and was thoroughly instructed on the skills of communication. While Victor was given the utmost attention, he never made it past learning basic and rudimentary skills. A similar case occurred in the 1970s in California, in which a child name "Genie" was found after being severely abused for 12 years (Rymer 1993). Scientists studied her in order to ascertain psychologically how the body allows for language acquisition. After working with Genie for many years, she was only able to learn to a certain level, and never progress, similar to Victor. What these two stories indicate is that biologically, they could learn language and communicate up to a certain level. However, because of their lack of socialization for so many years, they would never go beyond the point of what they learned.

Theories of Learning: Behaviorism and Social Learning

While our understanding of human development is rooted in sociology, we still need to give attention to the psychological aspects. There are certain actions, such as **behaviorism**, that are primarily found in psychology; but the concept still helps us to understand society as a whole. Behaviorism is a theory that came to prominence in the late nineteenth century, which claims that human behavior is rooted in biological processes (Baldwin 1986; Baldwin and Baldwin 1988; Dishion, McCord, and Poulin 1999). Famous psychologists such as B. F. Skinner (1904–1990), John Watson (1878–1958), and Ivan Pavlov (1849–1936) are well known for their experiments and findings on behaviorism. While behaviorism helps us to understand the relationship between rewards and punishments, **social learning** is more attuned to the sociological aspect of how individuals adapt their behavior (Baldwin 1986; Bandura 1977; Bandura and Walters 1963). Social learning takes behaviorism one step further by claiming that we model and moderate our behavior based on how we observe others observing us. In order to better understand how this is exemplified in society, let's take a look at socialization and symbolic interaction.

> **Behaviorism:** The theory that human and animal behavior can be explained in terms of conditioning, without appeal to thoughts or feelings.

> **Social Learning:** The view that people learn by observing others.

Socialization and Symbolic Interaction: The Effects of Social Learning

If you recall from Chapter 1, symbolic interactionism helps us to understand the relationship between language and gestures, small micro-interactions which help us to understand the larger picture. Symbolic interactionism and socialization share a very strong relationship in that the way we come to understand ourselves, the situation we are in, and how to respond or react, is rooted in symbolic interactionism. In doing this, we are able to develop our identities and alter them as the situation requires (Blumer 1969, 1970; Hutcheon 1999; Mead 1934, 1938). Charles Horton Cooley (1864–1929) understood this relationship and noted that this process is best understood as the looking-glass self—a way in which we interpret how others view us. Cooley noted that we are constantly engaged in this reflexive process, and how engaged we are in is often dependent on the groups that we are meeting to understand ourselves. He noted that there are two types of reference groups: primary and secondary.

Looking-Glass Self: The self-image an individual forms by imagining what others think of his or her behavior and appearance.

Primary groups are comprised of close, emotional, and interpersonal ties, such as family members, significant others, or close friends. Primary groups hold a huge amount of significance for us in how we understand ourselves in society since our relationship with them is predicated on strong bonds, and a sense

Primary Groups: A group of individuals living in close, intimate, and personal relationship.

that these individuals know us, sometimes, better than we know ourselves. Because of the strength of the bond we share with these individuals, we are more likely to alter our behavior regarding certain aspects. For example, imagine that you are going to ask out someone that you have had a huge crush on for quite some time, before you ask this person out, you might consult your best friend. If your best friend gives you their blessing, then you will proceed to ask your crush out; if not, you will begin to think at great length, if you should ask this person out on a date or not.

Secondary groups are slightly different in that they are reference groups we use to understand ourselves, but their bonds are not as strong. They tend to be comprised of large, impersonal, and often short-lived

Secondary Groups: A group of people with whom one's contacts are detached and impersonal.

relationships. Because of this, you will adjust your behavior slightly if you see that you are violating a norm with them, but you won't feel a deep sense of commitment in doing so. For example, your professor is a secondary group member in relation to you. Imagine that you speak out in class, a violation of the norms governing a classroom, your professor will tell you to be quiet and you will think momentarily whether your professor considers you to be rude, but after the class has ended, you will probably not think of this situation any further. However, if you are at a family gathering and you speak out at the dinner table or use harsh language, the way your parents and family react will stay with you much longer. Additionally, primary and secondary groups can comprise what is called a reference group—these are groups that you use to serve as a reference for societal standards. You may use your parents as a reference group for what is

Reference Groups: A group with which an individual identifies and whose values the individual accepts as guiding principles.

acceptable or not acceptable in a marriage, your professor as what is acceptable or not acceptable in terms of obtaining your degree, and your friends in what is acceptable or not acceptable regarding fashion or current popular vernacular. Primary, secondary, and reference groups are found within the agents of socialization and they assist in maintaining the norms within society.

Agents of Socialization

Agents of socialization are institutions that are found within all societies. At various levels and stages in our lives, they assist in the socialization process. The agents of socialization we will be discussing in this chapter are the family, education, peers, religion, mass and social media, and work. These agents work both independently and codependently in the socialization process throughout our lives.

Family

Family is the primary and most important agent of socialization. From the moment we are conceived until death, our families are the first and continual agent of socialization that we encounter. We begin to understand the world in which we live, the dynamics of relationships, expectations of gender roles, and other agents of socialization such as education, religion, and work, through our families. One of the trends that we have seen in society is the changing attitudes regarding marriage. According to the American Psychological Association, 40%–50% of couples divorce. Based on this rising trend, this may impact children's views on marriage and child-rearing. Additionally, class has a huge impact on family dynamics. Children who are raised in low socioeconomic households are often taught to obey, rather than question or challenge, authority. Consequently, children who are raised in middle- to upper-class households are taught to be creative, parents have opportunities to allow their children to focus on being children, rather than socializing them to enter the workforce, as lower class families tend to socialize their children (Kohn 1989; Lareau 2002).

Education

In addition to the family, the education system is a profound agent of socialization. This is where children leave the home and enter into a public sphere and begin socializing in new ways. From the structure of the school day, the assignments, and the expectations set forth by the teacher, the school offers opportunities for students to interact and socialize to expectations of society. One of the ways that this is accomplished is through the concept of the *hidden curriculum;* students are socialized in a subtle subconscious manner to the norms of the greater society. For example, many students do not like to work on group projects. Invariably, there will be one student who does all the work, another student who doesn't do any work, and the rest of the group. However, when a teacher gives a group of students a project, she is actually socializing them to such concepts as working collaboratively, conflict resolution, goal setting, and much more. Class is also present in the education system. Students attending schools in low socioeconomic areas are often lacking in resources, vocational opportunities, and have higher issues regarding safety (Bowles and Gintis 1976; Kozol 2005).

Peers

In sociology, we define peers as being individuals that are similar to you in aspects such as age and social class. As you age, your reliance on your peers as reflections of you and your actions become less. However, peers are probably most significant during the years of adolescence. Imagine, what your friends have to say about the clothes you wear, who you date, and what activities you are involved in hold more weight than other reference groups such as your parents or your teachers. Similarly, studies indicate that peer groups around this age tend to have their own set of norms and culture that may be different from that of the larger culture (Hine 2000; Sebald 2000). Therefore, we often find that adolescents will change their behavior, attitudes, even their clothing, food, and activity preference to suit that of their peer group; this is known as **anticipatory socialization**. It is a process that tends to weaken as individuals age.

Anticipatory Socialization: The process, facilitated by social interactions, in which nongroup members learn to take on the values and standards of groups that they aspire to join.

Religion

According to the Pew Forum (http://www.pewforum.org/religious-landscape-study/), over 75% of Americans have a religious affiliation. Theoretically, Durkheim presented the notion that individuals need a religion, or something similar, to believe in because it serves various functions in society. One function is that it brings people together, based on common bonds. It is also used to reinforce certain norms and values in society. For example, religion may instill certain values in a society such as kindness, willingness to help others or perhaps it instills certain norms such as attitudes toward killing. These aspects are often echoed by Parsons (1970) in which he further noted that religion acts as a reinforcement for socializing societies about values and beliefs, which contribute to a normative culture.

Mass and Social Media

No matter where we go and what we do, we are constantly connected. Whether you're in a classroom, a job setting, or even the doctor's office, you are constantly being bombarded with technology. Mass and social media are concepts that can be both good and bad—depending on how they are used. With the ever-increasing creation of new technology and ways to stay connected, we essentially have the world at our fingertips. Media allows us to be attuned to what is going on; however, it can also alter how we see ourselves, our involvement, and our attitudes toward any aspect in society. One of the topics that is usually discussed when examining media is magazines and billboards. Do we as a society allow these mediums to dictate how we dress, style, or see ourselves? Many will quickly answer "no" because we as a society are aware of the unrealistic standards set forth in advertising, but the  truth still shows up… mainly in our purchases or Instagram posts. We know that many of the models in magazines have been photo shopped, but they still sway our purchasing habits and impact how we look at ourselves and present ourselves in public. The fads and fashion trends that are present in media, whether it be clothing, the latest gadget, or challenge, we tend to participate in them because media socializes us too. Media and technology are not all bad. Years ago, when Facebook was invented, it allowed people from across the nation, or even the world, to remain in contact. Therefore, media can allow for strong social connections to remain.

Work

We spend most of our adult lives working. We see this practice as an opportunity to make more money, to invest in our futures; however, we do not tend to see work as a place for socialization. Our families and friends or peers have helped in socializing us into the person we are, but work socializes us in a more professional manner. We learn at work how to network with individuals, how to "dress the part" of a desire position we want, and how to reflexively see ourselves as a professional. These types of actions do not usually occur at home or with your friends. For  example, the types of conversations we have with our coworkers are more than likely going to adhere to a different set of norms than the conversations we have with our friends or family.

Total Institutions

When we engage in socialization, we are establishing our agency in dictating the process. For example, we choose which friends we hang out with, the weight of our parents' opinions, and so on. However, there are certain institutions, such as prisons, mental institutions, and armed services, that control the socialization process—these are known as total institutions. Typically, in the setting of a total institution, the members you come in contact with engage in a process of resocialization, where the norms you are accustomed to are now being broken down and a new set of norms is being established. For example, when someone joins the Army, everything that they know is now being challenged. They are taught to work for the unit, not for themselves, actions have different consequences, you are now a member of the Army—you are not the person you are before you joined. The intended purpose of a total institution is to resocialize you in such a manner that benefits you and the group. An individual can be a member of a total institution either voluntarily or involuntarily. For example, deciding to join the Army is a voluntary action; being incarcerated is not. Some individuals seek to resocialize themselves and therefore voluntarily commit themselves to a total institution. For example, an individual may commit themselves to a rehabilitation center to address mental and physical concerns. The process of resocialization is possible because the agents associated with institution reward individuals for positive behavior that subscribes to the norms set forth in the establishment. However, not every total institution is successful in the resocialization of individuals. Some argue that prisons are ineffective at resocializing individuals. Claims of higher rates of recidivism and prisoners learning the norms of the prison and the inmates rather than the norms of the society that they may return to one day. In fact, almost 50% of released inmates reenter the prison system (https://www.huffingtonpost.com/christopher-zoukis/report-documents-us-recid_b_9542312.html).

Total Institutions: A place of work and residence where a great number of similarly situated people, cut off from the wider community for a considerable time, together lead an enclosed, formally administered round of life.

Resocialization: The process by which one's sense of social values, beliefs, and norms are reengineered.

Interaction: The Process of Socialization

Socialization undeniably occurs through **social interaction**—these are words, body language, gestures, and other symbols that cue us into social norms in society. The process tends to be subtle and occurs in every moment of our lives. For example, when you are hanging out with your friends, you are cued into the social norms of what is acceptable by accolades that your peers give you, or even gestures. Consequently, we also take notice if someone is in violation of these norms and are thusly labeled as "weird" or "abnormal." According to Scheff (1966), violating these norms can range from being benign such as being labeled as "weird" all the way to extreme as someone being labeled as "dangerous." Imagine you are in an elevator, a person enters the elevator and rather than facing forward, as is the norm for society, the individual faces the back of the elevator. This is technically a violation of the social norm regarding proper elevator behavior—however this is not dangerous. Now imagine that you are in that same elevator and an individual gets on and stands very close to you, perhaps while trying to talk to you starts touching your arm are getting in your personal space. This behavior is a violation of a social norm and other members would consider it dangerous.

Social Interaction: Exchange between two or more individuals and is a building block of society.

Much of what we have been discussing so far can be summed up in the concept that socialization and social interaction are scripted concepts. Shakespeare said that "all the world's stage," Goffman furthered this concept by indicating that every social interaction is a script played on that stage. Goffman coined the term **dramaturgical approach** which essentially claims that everyday social interactions are based on a script which is governed by social norms. As with a stage in a theater, Goffman also indicated that society has stages. For example, in the **frontstage** of an interaction, we as **social actors** are concerned with properly carrying out the socially accepted script. In the **backstage**, we prepare for the script. The "character" that we create is usually through the process of understanding the presentation of self which ensures that we as social actors create impressions that our audience agrees with, thus allowing us to control a social situation. In order to ensure that we are successfully playing our roles, throughout the process we engage in what is known as impression management, and that includes the use of props—dress, voice fluctuations, gestures, and so on—to fully convince our audience that we are able to play this part. While this sounds a bit dramatic, let me provide some examples.

If I were to take on the role of a professor, my students—based on societal norms—would have certain expectations of how I should appear and conduct

Dramaturgical Approach: The elements of human interactions are dependent upon time, place, and audience; understood as part of the dramaturgical approach.

Frontstage: Actions are visible to the audience and are part of the performance.

Social Actors: Individuals who exercise agency.

Backstage: Behaviors when no audience is present; understood as part of the dramaturgical approach.

myself as a professor. They would expect me to dress professionally, be prepared for class, be punctual, and be confident as I lecture. If I were to show up late, wearing a bikini, not knowing what to cover in class that day, my students would doubt that I was suitable for this role. As a professor, I conduct myself very differently in the frontstage then I do in the backstage. For example, during the backstage phase of my interaction with students as a professor, I prepare my lecture notes, plan activities, and adjust my schedule so that I am punctual. While performing as a professor in the frontstage, I seem very calm, poised, and intelligent; what my students might not realize is that perhaps the topic we are discussing is not my area of specialization. Because I may sense their apprehension of my capabilities in addressing the topic, I reassure them that I have studied this topic before, I have conducted research, and so on—this is known as impression management, as I am managing the impression that my students may have of me. Goffman understands the dynamic fluidity of interaction that impacts how we present ourselves. As a result, Goffman saw the social self as a constant and changing product of our social interactions. Furthering this, Goffman indicated that as social actors, we have certain skills in our toolkit of dramaturgy that we are able to use at our disposal:

- Dramatic realization: This is an opportunity that many of us take to play up certain characteristics that we possess in order to be associated with those characteristics. For example, if you are really good at writing, you may display trophies earned for writing competitions on your desk or resume so that if anyone needs help with this task, they first think of you.
- Idealization: This is where we try to play up what we don't have in order to portray, ideally, if we had access to these resources, then we would have these items or opportunities. This is often seen in regard to socioeconomic status. Individuals who purchase items that are faux designer clothes or handbags, or buy name-brand items at outlet centers are an excellent example of this. They are trying to communicate through these props that they are in a higher socioeconomic category than they really are.
- Misrepresentation: This is often viewed as misdirection or perhaps to some, lying. These are encounters in which an unpleasant exchange has occurred and we try to misdirect our response so that we save face. For example, if your friend asks you if you like her boyfriend and you tell her that you like him better than the last—but don't fully disclose that you don't like this one either. Or if you tell your boss you are late because you got caught behind a train and it was really because you wanted to make a quick stop at Starbucks.
- Mystification: This concept refers to individuals who are largely unobtainable, such as CEOs or movie stars. Individuals who are high profile tend to create a persona that may be very different than their personal persona, such as when they are at home or with close friends. The motives for this ranges from protecting a brand that they promote or even to align themselves with the image of the company they work for.

Many of the aspects that assist in socialization are products of the culture that we live in. We do not often question certain norms that we adhere to, in fact we might not even know they are the norm, until we engage in other cultures. Therefore, to better understand socialization, we must also take a look at culture.

Culture

Culture is a wonderfully amorphous term that many use but may have difficulties in articulating exactly what it is. There are various things we consider to be culture: groups of people, geographic locations, popular culture, and so on. From the perspective of sociology, culture consists of beliefs, values, and norms that govern a group. Culture, just like social interactions, is very fluid. We can simultaneously say that we have culture while also creating culture. There are two broad aspects of culture that we use to define concepts and objects that we come in contact with in order to understand the norms, values, and beliefs in our culture: material culture and nonmaterial culture. Material culture is anything that is essentially tangible: the American flag, a piece of clothing, a compact disc. Nonmaterial culture is essentially abstract culture; it is culture that we can't touch but help us to understand or identify culture such as language and institutions. A material culture can also have nonmaterial cultural attributes. The American flag, for example, is material, but it represents a multitude of beliefs and values attributed to the American culture.

Additionally, sociologists also differentiate between ideal culture and real culture. Ideal culture is something that a culture professes to embrace, but perhaps the actions do not match the claim. In America, for example, we claim that we believe that everyone is beautiful no matter their height, weight, and size. However, social media indicates that this is not necessarily true. Real culture is what a culture actually embraces and exhibits. When we have a conflict between real and ideal culture, we are actually exhibiting cultural inconsistency.

Beliefs

Beliefs are best understood as ideas. They can be very persuasive in terms of collective behavior, or they can help identify certain cultures. For example, in America, the common belief that it is a land of opportunity and that it is a country where people can remake themselves. Beliefs are ideas that define and continue culture because societies tend to hold beliefs as facts and that because they are considered factual have the potential for consequences (Thomas and Thomas 1928). Examples of this are during the Salem Witch Trials, people were accused of being witches and therefore were subject to the consequences of that regardless of their affiliation with the occult. Or, when people thought that aliens had invaded the earth during Orson Welles's infamous radio broadcast in 1938.

Culture: Consists of the beliefs, behaviors, objects, and other characteristics common to the members of a particular group or society.

Material Culture: Refers to the physical objects, resources, and spaces that people use to define their culture.

Nonmaterial Culture: Intangible products created and shared between the members of a culture.

Ideal Culture: Values that a society professes to have.

Real Culture: Values that are actually present in a society.

Culture Inconsistency: The conflict between a society presenting ideal and real culture.

Beliefs: The tenets or convictions that people hold to be true.

Norms

Norms are best described rules in society—the proper way to behave. Some norms are explicitly taught such as your mother telling you not to chew with your mouth open at the dinner table. Other norms are just "known" in that they were never really taught, but by observing other people's behaviors in society, you adopt the norm. For example, no one told you how to stand in the elevator, such as which door to face, but whenever you get in an elevator everyone faces the same way.

> **Norms:** Social expectations that guide behavior.

Folkways

Folkways are considered to be weaker versions of norms, if you violate them, then the consequences—if any—are not severe. An example of this is to get in an elevator and stand the opposite way others are standing and take notes of their reaction. By doing this, you are technically violating a folkway. Nothing serious will happen, such as you won't receive a ticket for standing in the elevator facing a different direction—but people might stare at you.

> **Folkways:** Fairly weak norms that are passed down from the past.

Mores

Mores (pronounced MOR-ays) are considered to be strongly held norms and when you violate a more, the situation is considered to be quite offensive. Imagine you are standing in an elevator and you are talking loudly on a cell phone while eating food that happens to fall on the elevator floor. This scene is considered offensive or rude to many because in most societies, it is polite to hold a conversation with other elevator riders, but not in an obnoxious manner. It is also rude to spill food everywhere, potentially getting it onto other people's clothes as the room in an elevator is quite limited.

> **Mores:** Strongly held norms, the violation of which seriously offends the standards of acceptable conduct of most people within a culture.

Taboos

Taboos are considered to be very powerful mores and depending on the culture may even be considered unthinkable or inhumane. In the greater American culture, many might view the practice of polygamy, which is associated with Mormons, as being taboo. In other cultures, the practice of marrying young girls, known as child brides, is seen as taboo.

> **Taboos:** Powerful mores, violating them is considered to be a serious, even unthinkable, offense.

Laws

Laws are codified norms that are upheld by legal sanctions; they formally rationalize a society. An example of violating a law in an elevator is to pull the fire alarm when there isn't a threat of fire or danger.

Values

Values tend to be abstract and generalized standards in society; they often help in defining what a culture considers to be "right" and "wrong." Values almost act as unspoken codes that acts as a glue holding members in a culture together. In fact, Parsons (1951) indicated that values help to socially integrate a society.

Laws: Codified norms.

Values: Important and lasting beliefs or ideals shared by the members of a culture about what is good or bad and desirable or undesirable.

Beliefs	Understood ideas that are embodied within a culture
Norms	Social rules
Folkways	Weaker versions of norms with nonsevere consequences
Mores	Strongly held norms; violation of these are considered very offensive
Taboos	Powerful mores that are often considered inhumane
Laws	Codified norms
Values	Abstract standards in society

By examining culture, we need to look both at our own culture that we live in and also other cultures that are around the world. We tend to accept or reject other cultures based on how well they mesh with our culture. Our reactions tend to run the gamut when we examine other cultures and their differences. For example, in the United States, we drive on the right side of the road. In the United Kingdom, they drive on the left side of the road; this is different from our culture in the United States, but we don't feel threatened because it's not that different from our own culture. However, when other cultures are very different from our own, then we tend to display **ethnocentrism**—the belief that your culture is superior than another's. We tend to engage in this behavior because it is sometimes difficult to view other cultures from an **emic** perspective—looking from within to the outside. We tend to look at other cultures from an **etic** perspective—looking at a culture from the perspective of an outsider. As illustrated, certain practices such as driving on the

Ethnocentrism: The view that one's own culture is better than anyone else's culture.

opposite side of the road are not really difficult for us to comprehend because we tend to adopt an emic perspective to cultures similar to our own. When we look at cultures that may drastically be different, such as countries who have child brides, we tend to have an etic perspective because the concept of a child bride violates many of our cultures norms, beliefs, and values. Therefore, as a social practitioner, we must try to adopt the notion of cultural relativism, and look at other cultures through the lens of sociology.

Emic: From within the social group (from the perspective of the subject)

Etic: From outside (from the perspective of the observer).

Cultural Relativism: The principle of regarding the beliefs, values, and practices of a culture from the viewpoint of that culture itself.

Subcultures and Countercultures

As you can probably tell already, there isn't any one culture, or any one culture for one region or country. Multiple cultures reside in the same location. For example, if you are a Texan, you might say that you are Texan-American because you might identify with the Texan culture before identifying with the American culture. Additionally, there is culture associated with race, ethnicity, gender, age, profession, religion, and so on. Any one person can be a member of multiple cultures. In this instance, it is best to think of culture as a closet, in any one individual's closet is multiple sets of outfits, depending on the situation, you may wear a particular outfit. However, there are some situations in which people may wear two different outfits simultaneously, such as a blazer with jean—giving off the persona of a casual business outfit. This anecdote leads to the next discussion of subcultures, individuals who are simultaneously members of a culture that exists within and separately from a dominant culture. An example of this would be an individual whose parents are immigrants. The child may speak Spanish at home, but English in the classroom. Or she may engage in wearing ethnic clothing or eating ethnic food at home that she may not wear or eat outside of the home.

Subculture: Cultures that exist together within a dominant culture.

Counterculture: A way of life and set of attitudes opposed to or at variance with the prevailing social norm.

An individual who totally rejects, almost as if they are retreating from the dominant culture, is considered to be participating in a counterculture. There are different motives for why individuals may participate in countercultures. The most famous example would be the hippies from the 1960s. Hippies rejected the values, norms, and beliefs of the dominant American culture and tried to establish their new culture as a form of protest and separation from the mainstream establishment. Can you think of any countercultures that exist today?

Culture and Inequality

Culture and class have a dynamic relationship. Have you ever heard someone say, "ugh, they have no culture" and they are making a reference to someone's class standing? We have been socialized to associate certain cultures with class standing. This relationship is best exemplified by the teachings of Pierre Bourdieu. Bourdieu indicated that people understand each other based on the amount of capital they hold. The capital he is referring to is actually three types of capital: economic, social, and cultural. **Economic capital** refers to money, either the money an individual possesses or the ability to acquire more money. **Social capital** refers to the networks that an individual is able to gain access to thus allowing them gain economic or social mobility. And lastly, **cultural capital** refers to the accumulation of knowledge, abilities, and skills that an individual has. Combined, these capitals allow people to gain economic and social mobility thus improving their access and agency. In addition to these capitals, Bourdieu also discussed that we tend to associate people based on if their behavior, clothing, or activities are considered **high class** or **low class**. The relationship between class and capital is often ambiguous and amorphous. Because of this relationship with class, Bourdieu believes that if you are lacking in any of the capitals and you exhibit low class behavior, then your offspring will have the same disadvantages as you do; he refers to this as **social class reproduction**. This can be problematic because it may disallow individuals the ability to access opportunities. For example, a child has parents who did not graduate high school because they don't value education. They are exhibiting a culture that does not place an emphasis on education therefore that will be reproduced within the child because the child may look at his parents and note that even though his parents didn't have a formal education, they were still able to provide for him.

Economic Capital: Refers to money, property, and other assets.

Social Capital: Refers to networks of influence or support based on group membership.

Cultural Capital: Wealth in the form of knowledge, ideas, verbal skills, and the way an individual thinks or acts.

High Class: Activities or practices by groups or individuals with high socioeconomic class.

Low Class: Activities or practices by groups or individuals with low socioeconomic class.

Social Class Reproduction: Way in which status is reproduced from generation to generation.

Activity

In this chapter, we have discussed the process of socialization and the characteristics of culture. In examining these concepts, we have also discussed such concepts as norms, values, and beliefs. Complete the chart below based on your understanding of this chapter.

Agent of Socialization	Norms	Values	Beliefs
Family			
Education			
Peers			
Religion			
Mass and social media			
Work			

4 Social Interaction, Groups, and Formal Organizations

Social Interaction and Social Structure

Definitions

Very few people live in isolation. Throughout all of recorded history and across all known cultures, people have formed relationships with others. As the functionalists assert, some of these relationships are mutually beneficial (e.g., the relationship between buyers and sellers). In other cases, as is emphasized in conflict theory, these relationships may be exploitative (e.g., the relationship between military conquerors and the defeated). Regardless, **social interaction** is an unavoidable reality for most people.

Sociologists recognize that social interaction is not random. Rather, in every person's life, predictable patterns of social interaction based on social norms are evident. **Social structure** can be defined as *the normative relationships and patterns of interaction that guide group behavior in particular settings.* For example, the social structure in the Tidewater and Deep South plantations of colonial America established a distinction between male landowners, their wives, and their slaves, as well as norms for how these groups interacted. Likewise, the social structure in modern 21st-century grocery stores establishes a distinction between customers, front-line employees, and managers, as well as norms for how these groups interact. Social structure is useful because it helps us know what to expect and how to act in a variety of situations (e.g., at home, in the classroom, at work, at church, with friends while watching football, and with teammates while playing football).

Levels of Sociological Analysis

When describing social interaction and social structure, functionalists and conflict theorists tend to use the **macrosociology level of analysis**, while symbolic interactionists favor the **microsociology level of analysis**. This means while functionalists and conflict theorists tend to look at the broad functions or consequences of social structures, symbolic interactionists tend to focus more specifically on particular social rituals and how these "patterned social interactions" enhance the understanding of participants. For example, consider the social structure of American universities. A functionalist might conduct a macrosocial analysis of universities by considering the mutual benefits they have for both students and employers, with students earning credentials that qualify them for particular careers and employers benefitting from having a more qualified hiring pool. Likewise, a conflict theorist might conduct a macrosocial analysis of universities by considering how the high cost of tuition "weeds out" economically disadvantaged people from obtaining the credentials necessary to compete for high-paying jobs, thereby perpetuating status quo wealth inequality. On the other hand, a symbolic interactionist might conduct a microsocial analysis of universities by examining how the norms of social interaction within fraternities (e.g., "rushing," initiation, partying, and doing volunteer work for local charities) enhance the understanding of students regarding "what college is all about" and what their roles should be.

From *Introduction to Sociology* by Jason Hollar and Todd Martin. Copyright © 2018 by Kendall Hunt Publishing Company. Reprinted by permission.

Social Statuses and Social Roles

Social Status

Social status refers to the position a person occupies within a social structure. Examples of social statuses within the social structure known as *family* include mother, father, child, husband, and wife. Examples of social statuses within the social structure known as *a rock band* include the singer, the lead guitar player, the bass guitar player, the rhythm guitar player, and perhaps the keyboardist. Examples of social statuses within the social structure known as the United States of America include African American, Asian American, employed citizen, retired citizen, senator, representative, and president.

Social statuses affect the expectations we have of others. For example, in a family, we expect the mother and/or father to have a paying job, whereas we expect the child to go to a K-12 school (or perhaps be home-schooled). Social statuses also affect our sense of self. Imagine that somebody you have just met says, "So, tell me a little about yourself." Most likely, a significant part of your response would include sharing your social statuses. For example, you might say, "I am a nursing student, but until I complete my degree and get a job at the local hospital I will continue working as the produce manager at the local grocery store. I also am the mother of a two-year-old child, and I love to sing alto at First Methodist Church downtown." Notice that not one, but rather four social statuses were mentioned: nursing student, produce manager, mother, and alto singer. All of the many statuses a person has at a given time are that person's **status set**.

Ascribed statuses are assigned to individuals involuntarily. Examples include race, ethnicity, gender, and being somebody's son or daughter. Nobody chooses their ascribed statuses. Most often, we are simply born into them. On the other hand, **achieved statuses** are secured through effort and/or ability (Linton, 1936). Examples include being a college coach, a church member, a spouse, a janitor, a priest, a college student, and a parent. Often, there are visible signs that indicate a person's social status. These are called status symbols. Sometimes, **status symbols** are worn with pride (e.g., wedding rings announcing one's status as a husband or wife, ball caps announcing one's status as an Atlanta Falcons fan, bumper stickers announcing one's status as a "proud parent" or "American veteran"). At other times, status symbols are associated with shame (e.g., the uniform of a prisoner working on a road crew, or perhaps the moped of a person who has lost his license for driving drunk).

A **master status** is a status that has exceptional importance in a person's life, and greatly affects his or her other social statuses. An example of a master status is a person's gender. If you are a woman, that fact is likely to influence your self-image, where you work, how much money you make, where you shop, your choice of leisure activity, how you talk to other people, your voluntary social activities, and the groups to which you belong. Another example of a master status is a person's social class. If you are wealthy, that fact is likely to have an impact on all of the same areas previously mentioned regarding your gender.

Most often, the status set of an individual is fairly smooth and harmonious. However, sometimes some of the social statuses within a person's status set may be at odds with each other. This unfortunate situation is known as **status inconsistency**. For example, suppose a 14-year-old girl has a baby. The status "high school student" and the status "mother" may have trouble coexisting. The responsibilities of being a mother may necessitate that she drop out of extracurricular high school activities, may interfere with her high school social life, and may not allow her sufficient time for doing her homework.

Roles

Roles are the behaviors and privileges attached to particular social statuses. If you have trouble remembering the difference between social statuses and roles, remember the words of anthropologist Ralph Linton (1936): "A role represents the dynamic aspect of a status" (p. 119). In other words, while we *occupy* statuses, we *play* roles. For example, if your social status is *mother,* then some of your roles may include working to provide income for the family, taking care of the home, taking care of the children, and teaching the children. If your social status is *lead guitar player,* then some of your roles may include touring with the band, honing your skills through practice, and creating appropriate instrumental solos for the band's songs. If your social status is *employed American,* then some of your roles may include going to work, contributing a needed skill or service, paying income taxes, and paying social security.

Roles guide human interaction in a variety of settings. They guide behavior for clerks, customers, mothers, children, priests, parishioners, teachers, students, etc. Can you imagine how chaotic and frustrating life would be if everybody suddenly stopped playing their expected roles? The predictability that comes with playing normative social roles greatly enhances the efficiency and harmony of social interaction. With that being said, universal agreement on the roles associated with particular statuses is very rare (perhaps even nonexistent). For example, while some people believe the social status *mother* requires staying at home to create more time for housekeeping and meal preparation, others believe that it is more important for mothers to hold a job so they can contribute to the financial well-being of their family. Furthermore, even when there is agreement about *which* roles should be played, there may be different ideas about *how* these roles should be played. For example, one mother's idea about what constitutes supporting her children may be very different from another mother's idea. A person's beliefs about which roles should be associated with a particular status, as well as how these roles should be played out is known as **role performance**.

Role conflict refers to a situation in which a person discovers that a role associated with one social status is incompatible with that associated with another social status. For example, Betty's social status as a mother indicates if her child has a soccer game at 4:00 p.m. Monday afternoon, her role is to be at the soccer game to support him. However, Betty's social status as a restaurant manager indicates that if the restaurant inspector is coming at 4:00 p.m. Monday afternoon, her role is to be at the restaurant to answer questions and support her employees. She obviously cannot be at two different places at the same time, resulting in role conflict. **Role strain** refers to a situation in which a person discovers that two or more roles associated with a single social status are incompatible. For example, Judy's friend Alice is planning on wearing an outfit to a party that Judy thinks makes her look fat. As a friend, Judy feels that her role is to be supportive and encouraging, but as a friend she also feels that her role is to be honest. Telling Alice "You look amazing" would be supportive and encouraging, but not honest, while telling Alice "You look fat" would be honest but not supportive and encouraging. Thus, Judy is experiencing role strain. Because we have status sets consisting of multiple social statuses, each with a set of roles to play, occasional role conflict and role strain is probably inevitable.

As was previously mentioned, roles benefit society by enhancing the efficiency and harmony of social interaction. However, the following roles can also have a dark side. In a classic study commonly referred to as the Stanford Prison Study, Phillip Zimbardo (Zimbardo, 1972) found that humans are perhaps overly quick to let social statuses guide the roles they play. In this study, two dozen Stanford University volunteers were divided by a flip of the coin into guards and prisoners. Guards were told that they should create formal rules to maintain law, order, and respect during their 8-hour shifts. Prisoners were picked up in their homes by a real police officer, searched, cuffed, fingerprinted, and taken blindfolded to a simulated jail in the basement of the psychology building. The results were disturbing. Although Zimbardo had meant for the study to last 2 weeks, he had to end it after only 6 days because the guards were treating the prisoners like animals and the prisoners were acting like "dehumanized robots who thought only of escape, of their own individual survival, and of their mounting hatred for the guards" (Zimbardo, 1972, p. 4).

Reflection Questions: Statuses and Roles

1. What are some of your ascribed social statuses?
2. What are some of your achieved social statuses?
3. What are three roles you play for a particular social status?
4. Have you ever experienced role conflict? If so, please explain. Have you ever experienced role strain? If so, please explain.

Social Institutions

Social institutions can be defined as "the standard or usual ways that a society meets its basic needs" (Henslin, 2015, p. 104). Examples include (but are not limited to)

1. family,
2. government,
3. the educational system,
4. the economic system,
5. religion,
6. the health care system,
7. the legal system, and
8. the media.

Within all social institutions, people occupy different social statuses that entail particular roles. For example, social statuses within the economic institution include bankers, investors, business employees, engineers, entrepreneurs, and consumers. The role of bankers is to lend and manage money, the role of investors is to fund ideas and innovation, the role of business employees is to supply in-demand products, services, and jobs, the role of engineers and entrepreneurs is to improve and innovate products and services, and the role of consumers is to stimulate the economy by spending money.

Functionalist Perspective on Social Institutions

Because social institutions function to help society meet its basic needs, all societies have them. With that being said, in less developed societies they are often more informal and less structured than social institutions in the United States (Henslin, 2015). For example, while the educational institution in the United States requires over a decade of compulsory formal education for its children, the educational institutions in some of the more "primitive" cultures of South America, New Guinea, and Borneo only require the informal teaching of practical skills and cultural norms by parents or other tribe members.

Functionalists claim that there are five basic needs that social institutions help societies meet (Aberle et al., 1950; Mack and Bradford, 1979). If these five basic needs are not met, societies will not survive. These five **functional requisites** are:

1. replacing members who die or leave,
2. socializing new members,
3. producing and distributing goods and services,
4. preserving order, and
5. providing a sense of purpose.

The first two are met primarily by the family institution, although the educational system and religion also contribute to socializing new members. The need to produce and distribute goods and services is accomplished through the economic system. The need to preserve order is accomplished through the legal system (by both lawmakers and law enforcers, such as the police and the military). The need to provide a sense of purpose is accomplished primarily through religion, although the other social institutions also influence this.

Conflict Perspective on Social Institutions

Rather than benefitting all people equally, conflict theorists believe that social institutions primarily benefit those who have wealth, power, or prestige. Furthermore, conflict theorists assert that the main reason for this is because social institutions tend to be controlled by people who are already privileged in one of these three ways (Domhoff, 2006; Useem, 1984). For example, in many parts of the world (and sometimes even here in the United States), family decisions are left entirely to husbands, with wives and children having relatively no say in the matter. This creates a culture in which the family institution perpetuates male domination. Another example of how social institutions perpetuate the dominance of the privileged is the fact people who already have wealth, power, or prestige are more likely to hold upper leadership positions in large companies and in government.

Symbolic Interactionist Perspective on Social Institutions

Because symbolic interactionists use the microsociology level of analysis rather than the macrosociology level, they are less interested in how social institutions meet the basic needs of societies or how social institutions perpetuate the wealth, power, or prestige of the privileged. Rather, the focus of symbolic interactionists is on how face-to-face interactions within social institutions create a meaningful understanding of ourselves and our societies. For example, interactions with parents and siblings (in the family institution) and teachers and peers (in the educational institution) influence our beliefs about our strengths and weaknesses. Interactions with parents (in the family institution) and religious leaders (in the religious institution) influence our beliefs about what constitutes moral and immoral behavior. Interactions with college professors (in the educational institution) and leaders or supervisors (in the economic institution) influence our beliefs about what knowledge and skills are needed to become financially successful.

Dramaturgy

Symbolic interactionist Erving Goffman (1959) introduced the notion that people behave like actors on a theatrical stage. **Dramaturgy** is a theatrical concept used by sociologists to analyze social interaction as though participants are actors in the ongoing drama of life. Based on the nature and setting of the interaction, we assume a status (our *part* in the drama) and play out our social roles (our *lines* in the drama). For example, if you were a psychology student, dramaturgical analysis would consider "psychology student" to be your part. The behaviors expected of a psychology student (i.e., the social roles of a psychology student) would be viewed in dramaturgical analysis as your lines.

Reminiscent of Charles Horton Cooley's notion of the looking-glass self (1902), Goffman (1959; 1963) believed that in social interaction we imagine how others are judging our appearance and then react based on our feelings about these judgments. Thus, our behavior is guided by our desire to gain the advantages associated with making a favorable impression on others. Simply put, we want to show others what we think will impress them, and hide what we think will repulse or annoy them. **Impression management** is Goffman's term for the ways in which people use revelation and concealment to make a favorable impression on others. Using the language of dramaturgy, our **performances** are the product of impression management.

Dramaturgical analysis describes several elements of performance (Goffman, 1959). These include:

1. script (what we say)
2. costume (how we dress)
3. props (what we carry around), and
4. manner (voice tone, facial expression, posture, etc.).

For example, suppose you are at a job interview. Your script would be what you tell the search committee to convince them that you are the right person for the job. Your costume would be the professional-looking outfit that you wear to the interview. Your props might include a portfolio of your work that you bring to the interview. Your manner would be your pleasant voice tone and facial expression. All of these things together would comprise your performance.

Gender, idealization, and embarrassment also influence performance. In regard to gender (Goffman, 1976), the script, costume, and manner of women may differ from that of men because in societies that place high value on traditional ideas of femininity, women must be especially careful to avoid being judged as overly aggressive. In regard to idealization (Goffman, 1959), we construct our performances to try to convince ourselves and others that our intentions are admirable rather than selfish. For example, when asked, "Why do you want to be a doctor?" people tend to say things like "I've always wanted to help the sick" rather than "I want to make a ton of money." In regard to embarrassment (Goffman, 1956), this is the feeling of discomfort following a "spoiled performance." For example, you would feel embarrassment if you discovered your pants were unzipped while giving a speech. A related concept, **tact**, is when another person tries to help someone who is "messing up his performance" avoid embarrassment (e.g., by quietly and privately telling a man that his pants are unzipped).

Reflection Questions: Dramaturgy

1. Think of one of your social statuses and the social roles that go along with that status. In dramaturgical terms, what determines your part in the "drama of life"? What determines your lines?
2. Using the same example, consider your performance of your part and lines. What is your script? What is your costume? What are your props? What is your manner?
3. Using the same example, how might your gender affect your performance?
4. Using the same example, how might idealization affect your performance?

Ethnomethodology

Background assumptions are common understandings of how people are supposed to act. They are so deeply embedded within us that we are seldom even aware of them, and yet when they are violated we are left in a state of bewilderment (Henslin, 2015). For example, imagine how you would react if you were riding an elevator, and suddenly the lady next to you began loudly singing *The Star-Spangled Banner*. What if you were about to eat lunch at a fast food restaurant and a stranger took two bites of your cheeseburger? What would you do if your sociology instructor started lecturing in Spanish? The study of background assumptions, and how they help us make sense of our social worlds, is called **ethnomethodology**.

Harold Garfinkel (1967), the founder of ethnomethodology, asked his students to violate background assumptions. Some of his students would try to bargain with supermarket clerks, others would get within inches of people's faces and stare at them, and still others would address their parents as "Mr." and "Mrs." and ask permission to use the bathroom. Typical reactions included surprise, confusion, and even anger.

Reflection Questions: Ethnomethodology

1. Have you ever purposely violated a background assumption simply to see how people would react? What did you do? How did others react?
2. Have you ever had one of your background assumptions violated? How so? What did you do?

The Social Construction of Reality

Suppose you are walking through the parking lot of a large arena late at night, on your way back to your car after having attended a professional basketball game or a rock concert. You hear the sound of footsteps quickly approaching you. You turn around and see a disheveled man wearing an old flannel jacket over a dirty white t-shirt. He is holding a bottle of cheap wine. He is saying something to you, but you don't understand his speech. How will you respond? Will you ignore him? Will you give him some money? Will you ask him if he needs help? Suppose I told you that you had unknowingly dropped your car keys, and the man was simply trying to get you to stop so he could give them back to you. Did this possibility occur to you? If not, then the man's actual intentions would have had absolutely no bearing on your response. Rather, your response would have been entirely based on what you mistakenly believed to be the reality.

This example illustrates a principle known as **the Thomas theorem**. Named after the theorem's originators, sociologists William and Dorothy Thomas, the Thomas theorem states, "If men define situations as real, they are real in their consequences" (Thomas and Thomas, 1928, p. 572). In other words, the best predictor of what a person will do is his *belief* about the situation he is facing, even if that belief is mistaken. The actual reality of the situation is a far weaker predictor of what his response will be.

The Thomas theorem reminds us that what we perceive as reality is not based on objective reality, but rather on our socially constructed *beliefs* about reality. For example, there is no objective reality leading to universal disapproval of eating with your left hand. However, in Islamic cultures there is a **socially constructed reality** in which eating with your left hand is bad (as this is the hand associated with toileting in those cultures), just as there is a socially constructed reality in Christian cultures in which eating with your left hand is perfectly acceptable. In another example, while Americans might be tempted to declare that lukewarm soda is "just bad…plain and simple," in European countries soda is typically served with far less (if any) ice. What is perhaps even more surprising to many Americans is that rather than expressing a desire for our "wonderfully cold drinks," Europeans often disapprove of upping the ice ratio" (Bramen, 2011). When asked, they tend to make comments such as "Ice dilutes a drink" or "Who knows where that ice came from? It's probably dirty." Their socially constructed reality about the desirability of ice in drinks clearly differs from ours!

Social Groups

To truly understand what a social group is, it is helpful to distinguish a group from an aggregate and a category. An **aggregate** is a collection of people who simply happen to be at the same place at the same time (e.g., people waiting in line to buy tickets to an amusement park). Although they are physically together, people in an aggregate do not have sense of belonging together, and they will soon go their separate ways. A **category** is a collection of people, objects, or events that have similar characteristics (e.g., Roman Catholics, pickup trucks, and religious holidays). As with aggregates, members of a category do not necessarily have a sense of belonging together. In contrast with an aggregate and a category, a **group** is a collection of people who

1. think of themselves as belonging together,
2. interact with each another in patterned ways, and
3. have something in common.

Examples of groups include the president's family, members of a particular church, and students enrolled in a particular section of Introductory Sociology at a particular college or university.

Different Types of Groups

The different types of groups include primary groups, secondary groups, in-groups, out-groups, and reference groups. **Primary groups** are people who regularly interact and have close and enduring relationships (e.g., family members). **Secondary groups** are people who interact on a formal and impersonal basis to accomplish a specific objective (e.g., a group of professors at a college and a group of students taking a course together). Secondary groups tend to be more temporary than primary groups. For example, while family members tend to remain in the group for their entire lives (except in the case of divorce), professors at a college constantly change as old ones exit the group when they retire while new ones join the group when they are hired.

In-groups are the groups toward which people feel a sense of belongingness and loyalty, while out-groups are those toward which people feel antagonistic (Henslin, 2015). For example, if you are a student at the University of North Carolina at Chapel Hill (or simply a fan of their basketball team), your in-group is the UNC Tarheels while your out-group is the Duke University Blue Devils. Distinguishing between in-groups and out-groups not only enhances in-group harmony as people unite to fight a common enemy, but it also enhances hostility toward the out-group.

In a classic study commonly referred to as the Robber's Cave study, Muzafer Sherif and his colleagues (1956; 1961) studied the effects of competition and cooperation on conflict between in-groups and out-groups. Boys going to a summer camp (at Robber's Cave State Park in Oklahoma) were randomly assigned to two groups. The two groups were kept separate for a week and then they began to meet for a series of competitive games. Later, they had to work together to solve various problems (e.g., fixing a problem with the water supply). Results indicated that although competition seemed to intensify the rivalry between the two groups, cooperation seemed to diminish it. The implication is that if you want to improve the relationship between in-groups and out-groups, you need to get them to cooperate in pursuit of a common goal. For example, fighting on the same team against Germany, Japan, and Italy may have contributed to a decrease in American prejudice against the British and vice versa.

Reference groups are the groups we refer to when we are evaluating ourselves or trying to make a decision. For example, in order to judge our skill at basketball, we will consider the various skill levels of other basketball players on our team (our reference group) and try to decide how we measure up. We might conclude, "I block shots better than any of them. On the other hand, most of the others are better at free throws and outside shots. I'm about par for the course with dribbling and passing. Overall, I guess I'm a fairly average player." As a second example, suppose you are thinking about buying a car. Your reference group might be your friends, as you allow their opinions and vehicle purchases influence your own decision. You might think, "Eric says that he really likes his electric car because he doesn't ever have to spend money on gas or engine repairs. Maybe I should seriously consider going electric!"

Reflection Questions: Social Groups

1. Can you think of other examples of primary groups and secondary groups?
2. Can you think of other examples of in-groups and out-groups?
3. What are the implications of Sherif's Robber's Cave study (1956, 1961) on the conflict and animosity often seen between Muslims, Jews, and Christians?

Social Networks

All of the people that you know are linked to you and often to each other in what sociologists refer to as a **social network**. Your social network might include your family, coworkers, friends, fellow students, neighbors, and people you know from church. Not only do they all know you, but many of them know each other. Imagine creating a visual image of your social network by writing your name in the center of a tremendously large piece of paper, writing the name of everybody else you know around your name, and then drawing lines between the names of everybody who knows each other. This image would resemble a spider's web in its complexity.

Have you ever heard the saying, "We are all divided by just six degrees of separation"? This notion asserts that if you listed everybody in your social network, and then all of those people listed everybody in their social network, and then each of those people did the same, and so on, the names of everybody in the United States would be recorded by a chain of just six iterations. Among sociologists, this notion that everybody is linked by short chains of acquaintances is known as **the small-world phenomenon** (Kleinberg, 2000). Stanley Milgram (1967) tested the small-world phenomenon by creating two letters to be sent to "targets" in Massachusetts. The target of the first letter was the wife of a divinity student in Cambridge, while the target of the second letter was a stockbroker in Boston. Milgram then gave the first letter to volunteers from Wichita, Kansas, and the second letter to volunteers from Omaha, Nebraska. None of the volunteers knew the targets in Massachusetts. Milgram asked the volunteers to send the letter to someone they knew on a first-name basis who they thought might know the target. Each person who was given the letter from a previous recipient was asked to do the same, until the letter reached the target. Results indicated that the letters reached the two targets in an average of only six jumps, leading to the notion of "six degrees of separation."

Formal Organizations

Formal organizations are secondary groups that are formally organized to achieve specific goals. Examples include telephone companies, hospitals, and colleges. Etzioni (1975) describes the following types of formal organizations:

1. voluntary (e.g., churches, the Boy Scouts of America, the United Way),
2. coercive (e.g., prisons and mental hospitals), and
3. utilitarian (e.g., the company you work for).

People freely join voluntary organizations to accomplish goals that are personally and/or socially rewarding, while people are forced to join coercive organizations. Utilitarian organizations are joined for practical reasons, such as to earn money or a degree.

Bureaucracy

A bureaucracy is a large-scale formal organization that uses rules, a hierarchical structure of authority, and a clear division of labor in an effort to enhance efficiency. Examples of bureaucracies include universities, hospitals, banks, and large corporations such as IBM and General Motors. Max Weber (1968) describes the following six characteristics of bureaucracies:

1. **specialization and division of labor** (For example, at a hospital, the medical transcriptionist is only responsible for transcribing medical documents, the cardiologist is only responsible for treating heart problems, the anesthesiologist is only responsible for administering anesthesia to patients undergoing surgery, and the housekeeping staff is only responsible for keeping the rooms and equipment clean. Nobody tries to do other people's jobs, but rather they all just focus doing their own jobs.)
2. **hierarchical structure** (There is a clearly defined hierarchical chain of command from the bottom to the top. Because everybody knows the chain of command, they know exactly who to go to when they need direction, have questions, or have grievances.)
3. **written documents and files** (Everything is recorded in writing. This includes job descriptions, policies, goals and objectives, performance outcomes, minutes from meetings, employee files, and finances.)
4. **explicit qualifications for jobs** (People are not hired or promoted simply because the search committee has a good feeling about them. Rather, nearly every position within the company

requires specific education, training, and/or experience. For example, a full-time position as a sociology instructor at a North Carolina community college typically requires a Master of Arts degree in sociology and at least 2 years of teaching experience.)
5. **emphasis on the job rather than the person** (The general expectation is that employees do their jobs correctly and on time. This may require staying extra hours or working from home. If employees are unable to complete their duties successfully, they are replaced as quickly as possible.)
6. **emphasis on written rules** (The rules are in writing, in order to enhance everybody's awareness of them and in order to enhance the consistency with which they are enforced.)

Although the characteristics of bureaucracies succeed at increasing their efficiency, there are also problems associated with bureaucracies. Some of these are:

- bureaucratic alienation (Henslin, 2015): The emphasis on job duties rather than employee needs can make employees to feel more like cogs in a machine rather than human beings;
- bureaucratic ritualism (Merton, 1949): The emphasis on written rules and procedures may cause employees to care more about rules and procedures than fulfilling the goals of the bureaucracy (e.g., a special education teacher who is so focused on getting all the required paperwork submitted that she never gets around to helping her students improve academically);
- "Parkinson's Law" (Parkinson, 1955): This is the notion that bureaucratic employees must give the appearance of being busy even if they are not doing anything substantial, because if they appear otherwise they may be given extra work or be fired; and
- "The Peter Principle" (Peter and Hull, 1969): This is the notion that in bureaucracies, people are promoted for doing a good job until they reach their level of incompetence (e.g., an excellent produce manager at a franchise grocery store is promoted and becomes an excellent store manager, and then he is promoted again and becomes a rather poor district manager).

Group Dynamics

How do groups affect us? How do we affect groups? How does each member of the group affect each other member? **Group dynamics** refers to the reciprocal influence that groups and individuals have on each other, as well as the influence that particular members of the group have on each other.

The size of the group matters. Simmel (1950) found that small groups with two or three people tend to be the most intense, the most informal, and the most unstable (because the departure of just one or two people can destroy the group). As group size increases, the intensity of the relationships tends to decrease while formality (e.g., the presence of formal roles and objectives) and stability tend to increase.

The size of the group also seems to have an effect on willingness to help others. In a study in which participants in a booth were tricked into believing that they were in groups of different sizes (they actually heard recorded messages but thought they were hearing other group members communicating with them from the other booths), Darley and Latane (1968) found that willingness to help a group member who appeared to be having a seizure decreased as perception of group size increased. When participants believed the size of the group was two (just the participant and the person who appeared to be having the seizure), 100% left their booth and tried to help the person they thought was in the other booth. When participants believed the size of the group was three, 80% tried to help. When they believed the size of the group was six, only 60% tried to help. The decreased likelihood that people in larger groups will volunteer to help compared to people in smaller groups is called **diffusion of responsibility**.

People in groups also tend to value consensus, and thus may avoid challenging the ideas of other group members. Solomon Asch's classic experiment on group conformity (1952) is a great example of this hesitance to challenge the consensus of the group. Irving Janis (1972) defined **groupthink** as "A mode of thinking that people engage in when they are deeply involved in a cohesive in-group, when the members' strivings for unanimity override their motivation to realistically appraise alternative courses of action" (p. 9). More simply, groupthink occurs when people in the group come to a consensus prematurely without adequate consideration of what could go wrong or better alternatives. Groupthink often results in very poor decisions. As examples of groupthink fiascos, Janis (1972; 1982) discusses U.S. failure to anticipate the bombing of Pearl Harbor, the failed 1961 Bay of Pigs invasion of Cuba, and failed 1980-hostage rescue in Iran.

Leadership

Although we tend to think of formal groups such as businesses and college classes when we hear the term *leader*, even informal groups of friends (cliques) usually have leaders. Leadership is a group process in which one or several members are able to influence the goals and behaviors of a group more than the rest.

There are three basic leadership styles (Lippitt and White, 1958):

1. Authoritarian leadership,
2. Democratic leadership, and
3. Laissez-faire leadership.

Authoritarian leaders give orders and direct activities without soliciting input from other members of the group (e.g., a drill sergeant telling privates in basic training to do 50 push-ups). **Democratic leaders** set the agenda and ultimately make the decisions, but solicit and value the opinions of the other team members (e.g., a governor who solicits the input of his advisors prior to giving an executive order in response to a state emergency). **Laissez-faire leaders** neither set the agenda nor try to direct followers in an obvious way (e.g., a CEO who plays a lot of golf and only stops by the office to "rubber stamp" whatever actions the Vice President, Chief Financial Officer, and other company executives recommend). Although the democratic leadership style is usually the best, the other two styles may work in certain situations. Life or death situations, which require an immediate response (e.g., a person choking to death or soldiers under attack), may require an authoritarian leader who is willing to quickly take charge and tell people exactly what to do. Laissez-faire leadership may be the best style in situations where the other members of the group are highly motivated and skilled, while the official leader is less motivated and skilled (e.g., a CEO within 2 years of retirement who sees himself more as a source of support than a decision-maker, because he realizes that his skill set is "behind the times" and is ready to turn the reigns of the company over to the "hungry young minds of the future").

The Power of Authority: The Milgram Experiment

Regardless of whether we are talking about parents, high school principals, preachers, managers, CEOs, or presidents, formal leaders are in a position of authority. As such, they have considerable influence over other group members. There are two important implications to this fact:

1. Leaders need to be very careful about what they say and do, and
2. We need to be very careful about who we choose to put into leadership roles.

Stanley Milgram's research on the power of authority (1963; 1965) at Yale University supports these two implications in a dramatic way!

The purpose of Milgram's obedience study was to determine the extent to which people will inflict pain on others in obedience to the instructions of an authority figure. Volunteers assigned to be "teachers" thought that they were giving electric shocks to "learners" for incorrect recall of word pairs, using a machine with controls arranged left to right from 15 to 450 volts. However, unknown to the teachers, the learners were only pretending that they were receiving shocks. The learners would moan at 75 volts, shout to be let out at 150 volts, scream at 270 volts, and go dead silent after 330 volts. All the teachers were told in regard to their protests about the suffering of the learners was "The experiment requires that you continue." Results indicated that none of the 40 volunteers assigned to be teachers stopped before the 300-volt level, and two-thirds of the teachers (26 out of 40) went all the way to 450 volts. Evidently, people tend to obey authority figures even when told to hurt others. Similarly, most of Hitler's Gestapo agents, concentration camp guards, and soldiers simply did whatever they were told to do. If they were later arrested for war crimes, they often protested they were "just doing their jobs."

Reflection Questions: Group Dynamics

1. Can you think of examples of times when groupthink led to a poor decision in a group of which you were a part?
2. Can you think of examples of times when you have obeyed a person who had authority over you even when that person was trying to get you to do something that might be considered immoral or illegal?
3. Do you have any leadership roles? If so, what style of leadership do you think you use? Why?
4. What are the implications of the results of Milgram's obedience study (1963; 1965) on the Abu Ghraib torture and prisoner abuse scandal?

References

Aberle, D. F., A. K. Cohen, A. K. David, M. J. Leng, and F. N. Sutton. 1950. "The Functional Prerequisites of a Society." *Ethics* 60 (2): 100–11.

Asch, S. 1952. Effects of group pressure upon the modification and distortion of judgments. In *Readings in Social Psychology*. Edited by G. E. Swanson, T. M. Newcomb, and E. L. Hartley, 2–11. New York, NY: Holt, Rinehart, and Winston.

Bramen, L. August 12, 2011. Why Don't Other Countries Use Ice Cubes? *Smithsonian.com.* https://www.smithsonianmag.com/arts-culture/why-dont-other-countries-use-ice-cubes-50361097

Cooley, C. H. 1902. *Human Nature and the Social Order.* New York, NY: Charles Scribner's Sons.

Darley, J. M., and B. Latane. 1968. "Bystander Intervention in Emergencies: Diffusion of Responsibility." *Journal of Personality and Social Psychology* 8 (4): 377–83.

Domhoff, W. G. 2006. *Who Rules America? Power, Politics, and Social Change.* 5th edition. New York, NY: McGraw-Hill.

Etzioni, A. 1975. *A Comparative Analysis of Complex Organizations: On Power, Involvement, and Their Correlates.* New York, NY: Free Press.

Garfinkel, H. 1967. *Studies in Ethnomethodology.* Englewood Cliffs, NJ: Prentice Hall.

Goffman, E. 1956. "Embarrassment and Social Organization." *American Journal of Sociology* 62 (3): 264–71. http://www.d.umn.edu/cla/faculty/jhamlin/4111/Readings/GoffmanEmbarrassment.pdf

Goffman, E. 1959. *The Presentation of Self in Everyday Life.* Garden City, NY: Doubleday.

Goffman, E. 1963. *Stigma: Notes on the Management of Spoiled Identity.* Englewood Cliffs, NJ: Prentice Hall.

Goffman, E. 1976. "Gender Display." *Studies in the Anthropology of Visual Communication* 3 (2): 69–77. http://www.csun.edu/~snk1966/Goffman%20Gender%20Display.pdf

Henslin, J. M. 2015. *Essentials of Sociology: A Down-to-Earth Approach.* 11th edition. Upper Saddle River, NJ: Pearson.

Janis, I. L. 1972. *Victims of Groupthink: A Psychological Study of Foreign-Policy Decisions and Fiascos.* Oxford: Houghton-Mifflin.

Janis, I. L. 1982. *Groupthink: Psychological Studies of Policy Decisions and Fiascos*. Boston, MA: Houghton Mifflin.

Kleinberg, J. 2000. The small-world phenomenon: An algorithmic perspective. In *Proceedings of the 32nd ACM Symposium on the Theory of Computing*, 163–70. https://www.cs.cornell.edu/home/kleinber/swn.d/swn.html

Linton, R. 1936. *The Study of Man*. New York, NY: Appleton-Century-Crofts.

Lippitt, R., and R. K. White. 1958. An experimental study of leadership and group life. In *Readings in Social Psychology*. Edited by E. E. Maccoby, T. M. Newcomb, and E. L. Hartley, 496–511. New York, NY: Holt, Rinehart, and Winston.

Mack, R. W., and C. P. Bradford. 1979. *Transforming America: Patterns of Social Change*. 2nd edition. New York, NY: Random House.

Merton, R. K. 1949. *Social Theory and Social Structure*. Glencoe, IL: Free Press.

Milgram, S. 1963. "Behavioral Study of Obedience." *Journal of Abnormal and Social Psychology* 67 (4): 371–8.

Milgram, S. 1965. "Some Conditions of Obedience and Disobedience to Authority." *Human Relations* 18 (1): 57–76.

Milgram, S. 1967. "The Small World Problem." *Psychology Today* 1 (1): 61–7. http://snap.stanford.edu/class/cs224w-readings/milgram67smallworld.pdf

Parkinson, C. N. November, 1955. "Parkinson's Law." *The Economist*, 1–5. http://www.economist.com/node/14116121

Peter, L. J., and R. Hull. 1969. *The Peter Principle: Why Things Always Go Wrong*. New York, NY: William Morrow and Company.

Sherif, M. 1956. "Experiments in Group Conflict." *Scientific American* 195 (5): 54–8. http://patrick-fournier.com/d/cours13-6607.pdf

Sherif, M., O. J. Harvey, B. J. White, W. R. Hood, and C. W. Sharif. 1961. *Intergroup Conflict and Cooperation: The Robber's Cave Experiment*. Norman, OK: University of Oklahoma Book Exchange. http://psychclassics.yorku.ca/Sherif/chap1.htm

Simmel, G. 1950. *The Sociology of Georg Simmel*. Edited and translated by K. H. Wolff. Glencoe, IL: Free Press. https://archive.org/stream/sociologyofgeorg030082mbp/sociologyofgeorg030082mbp_djvu.txt

Thomas, W. I., and D. S. Thomas. 1928. *The Child in America: Behavior Problems and Programs*. New York, NY: Alfred A. Knopf.

Useem, M. 1984. *The Inner Circle: Large Corporations and the Rise of Business Political Activity in the U.S. and U.K.* New York, NY: Oxford University Press.

Weber, M. 1968. *Economy and Society: An Outline of Interpretive Sociology*. Edited and translated G. Roth, and C. Widdich. Berkeley, CA: University of California Press.

Zimbardo, P. G. 1972. "Pathology of Imprisonment." *Society* 9 (6): 4–8.

5 Social Stratification

Power, Wealth, and Prestige

As conflict theorists emphasize and most of us know from personal experience, we do not all have the same opportunities. Max Weber (1947, 1968) asserts that this inequity of opportunities can be the result of:

1. power inequities,
2. property (henceforth referred to as *wealth*) inequities, and
3. prestige inequities.

Power is the ability to control others, even against their will. An example of the impact of power inequities can be seen by contrasting political opportunities for women in the United States with political opportunities for women in Afghanistan in the late 1990s. At the same time Madeleine Albright was serving as the U.S. secretary of state under Bill Clinton, women living in Taliban-governed Afghanistan were denied the right to hold any political offices. **Wealth** is the total value of one's property and money, minus one's debt. While many people believe wealth is synonymous with income, it is possible to have low wealth and high income if you owe a lot of money despite having a large salary, or high wealth and low income if you own valuable property without debt (e.g., 100 acres of land, paid in full) despite having a small salary. **Prestige** is the respect and admiration afforded to an individual due to a socially valued personal achievement, quality, or status. An example of the impact of wealth and prestige inequity can be seen by contrasting educational opportunities for the children of U.S. presidents with the children of working- or middle-class Americans. Going back at least as far as John F. Kennedy, the children of U.S. presidents have attended expensive, high-prestige universities such as Georgetown, the University of Pennsylvania, Brown, and Stanford (Jackson, 2017), while the children of working-class or middle-class parents are more likely to attend less-expensive community colleges or "low to moderate prestige" 4-year colleges and universities.

Social stratification refers to the division of people into categories based on their relative power, wealth, and prestige. While social stratification exists in all societies, there are differences in which of the three factors of inequality (power, wealth, and prestige) has the most impact. For example, in communist nations such as China, Cuba, and Vietnam, the primary determinant of social stratification is power, whereas in capitalist nations such as the United States wealth plays a larger role. Incidentally, prestige contributes to social stratification in both communist and capitalist countries. This is largely due to the fact that people tend to admire both the powerful and the wealthy (Henslin, 2015), although there are exceptions to this trend. For example, most people do ***not*** admire international drug lords, resulting in low prestige for this group despite high power and wealth.

Systems of Social Stratification

Social mobility is the extent to which a person can move to a more- or less-privileged category on the social stratification system. Three types of social mobility include **intergenerational mobility** (where social class changes within a family from one generation to the next), **structural mobility** (where large numbers of people within a society change their social class due to social changes, as was the case for American women as they began to gain more legal rights and suffer less discrimination in American society), and **exchange mobility** (where one group of people move down in social class while another move up).

The four major systems of social stratification are slavery, caste, estate, and class. Social mobility differs significantly between these four systems. In **closed systems** (e.g., slavery and caste systems), the boundaries between social stratification categories are firm, resulting in very little social mobility. In **open systems** (e.g., the class system), the boundaries are less firm, allowing sufficient social mobility for people to change their power, wealth, or prestige.

Slavery

In a slave system, there are two distinct categories of people:

1. free people, and
2. slaves.

Slaves are the legal property of free people. People can be enslaved due to getting defeated in war, owing debt, or having committed a crime. In some societies, slaves have had limited legal rights. For example, Roman slaves had the right to buy their freedom, which was the most common way in which the small minority of Roman slaves who achieved their freedom did so (Cartwright, 2013). With that being said, the vast majority of slaves have no power, own no property, and are regarded by others as "the bottom rung of the social ladder." Examples of slave systems include Ancient Egypt, Ancient Greece, Ancient Rome, and the Tidewater and Deep South sections of the United States prior to the Civil War. Although legally banned throughout the world, slavery continues to occur in parts of sub-Saharan Africa and central Asia (Hess and Frohlich, 2014; Rezaian, 2017).

Caste

In a caste system, people are born into a particular social stratification category known as one's **caste**. Membership in that caste is lifelong, and marriage between people of different castes is strictly forbidden. As such, the caste system is an example of a totally closed system. Social status is ascribed (completely determined by parental status) rather than achieved through effort. The best known example of a caste system is traditional India, which had five castes:

1. the Brahmins (priests and scholars),
2. the Kshatriyas (rulers and soldiers),
3. the Vaisyas (merchants),
4. the Shudras (peasants and craftworkers), and
5. the Dalits (those who did degrading work such as cleaning latrines or handling dead bodies).

Although included here as a fifth caste, the Dalits (or "untouchables") were considered to be so lowly that they were typically viewed as being outside of the caste system. Although the Indian caste system was formally abolished in 1950, and is being gradually replaced with a social class system based on material wealth, the caste system continues to serve as a guide to behavior for some people within that nation (BBC News, 2017; Polgreen, 2011). In addition to the Indian caste system, the apartheid system in South Africa and the system of segregation in the southern part of the United States between the end of the Civil War and the Civil Rights Movement of the 1960s are often cited as examples of caste systems. In the case of South African apartheid and segregation in the southern United States, caste was determined by race, with whites afforded more power and prestige than blacks.

Estate

In an estate system, which was dominant in Europe during the Middle Ages and the Renaissance, power was primarily welded by religious and political elites. The three legally defined estates in medieval Europe were:

1. the clergy,
2. the nobility, and
3. the commoners.

The clergy (e.g., the Roman Catholic Church) had great political power, owned land, and gained wealth from tithes that they imposed on anybody who lived within the boundaries of a parish. The nobility included privileged, "titled" families (e.g., dukes, lords, earls). Like the clergy, the nobility had political power and influence, owned large amounts of land, and gained wealth from it even though they did no farming themselves (Anderson, 2008a; Henslin, 2015). The commoners included peasant farmers (who often toiled on land owned by the nobility), artisans, merchants, traders, and townspeople. Estate systems resulted in extreme inequality, as most peasants were extremely poor while the highest ranking members of the clergy and nobility were usually quite wealthy. However, there were more opportunities for limited social mobility within the estate system than there were within the slave or caste systems. Some commoners succeeded in acquiring wealth and were even able to purchase titles, whereas other commoners married into more privileged lifestyles (Anderson, 2008b; Thompson and Hickey, 2007).

Class

In a class system, the primary determinant of one's social class is money and/or material possessions. Typically, the social classes are labeled:

1. the upper class,
2. the middle class, and
3. the working class.

One's social class can be an ascribed status, an achieved status, or a bit of both. Although people are born into a particular social class (just as members of a slave system, caste system, or estate system are born into a social stratification category), the class system is by far the most open of the four systems of social stratification. Anybody who succeeds in gaining enough wealth can move into a higher social class, just as anybody who loses enough wealth can move into a lower social class.

Despite the increased possibility of social mobility compared to the other systems, the class system still contains a great deal of inequality. Typically, a small upper class own the majority of a class-based nation's assets and has a disproportionate level of influence and power. In fact, worldwide, the level of wealth and power inequality seems to be increasing. According to Rothkopf (2008), the world's wealthiest people now form a *global superclass* of about 6,000 people. The richest 1,000 of this superclass possess more wealth than the poorest 2.5 billion people on the planet. The wealthiest 1% of adults worldwide own about 40% of the Earth's wealth, while the wealthiest 10% own about 85% of the world's wealth.

Determinants of Social Class

As was mentioned at the beginning of this chapter, Max Weber (1947, 1968) asserted that social stratification is the result of differences in three areas: wealth, power, and prestige. It is important to note that people aren't necessarily equal in these three areas. For example, college professors usually have higher prestige than accountants, while accountants usually have higher incomes. Local officials in the former Soviet Union often had lots of power, but much less wealth and prestige. Also, as was previously mentioned, drug lords often have lots of power and wealth, but lack prestige. **Socioeconomic status** is a ranking of social class that combines income, occupational prestige, level of education, and neighborhood in an attempt to assess people's positions in the social stratification system.

Reflection Questions: Social Class

1. Why does social stratification continue to exist in communist nations despite the fact that the level of wealth inequity decreased significantly after the government took control of privately owned, "for profit" industries? *(Hint: Consider how might Max Weber's views on social class [1947, 1968] might be relevant to this question.)*
2. Sociologists assert that our class position affects almost everything we think and do. How might social class affect our religious beliefs and our political affiliation?
3. How might social class affect whether or not we vote?
4. How might social class affect the foods we eat, the clothes we wear, the television shows we watch, and whether or not we own a computer?
5. How might social class affect our health, happiness, and how long we live?

The Functionalist Perspective on Social Stratification

The Davis-Moore Theory

Functionalists believe that characteristics that are typical of all societies tend to recur because they have beneficial functions. Because all societies contain social inequality, perhaps it too serves some important purpose. Kingsley Davis and Wilbert Moore (1945) offered the most well-known theory of why social stratification is beneficial to society. The Davis-Moore theory asserts that society requires a wide variety of jobs. Some of them are highly technical, difficult, or stressful (e.g., a rocket scientist, a brain surgeon, an army general), whereas others are less technical, less difficult, and less stressful (e.g., an assembly-line worker, a street sweeper). Davis and Moore believed that in order to attract talented people to the more demanding jobs, it is necessary to offer extra pay, power, or prestige. Otherwise, many people who could have succeeded at the more demanding jobs would instead choose easier jobs requiring less education or training, resulting in too many lower-level, unskilled workers and too few upper-level, highly skilled workers.

Tumin's Critique of the Davis-Moore Theory

Melvin Tumin (1953) offered the following three criticisms of the Davis-Moore theory of social stratification:

1. The theory's assertion that society gives the most pay and prestige to the most important jobs is questionable. Despite the fact that garbage collectors and elementary school teachers have low pay and fairly low prestige, while professional baseball players have very high pay and prestige, one could argue that garbage collectors save lives by helping prevent the spread of disease and teachers help students learn knowledge and skills that will significantly improve the quality of their lives, while professional baseball players provide society with something that is far less important—entertainment;
2. The Davis-Moore theory does not consider the fact that lack of sufficient money for tuition, boarding, and books can prevent many talented people from being able to earn the college credentials necessary for obtaining high-pay, high-prestige jobs. Therefore, for working-class

and middle-class people, simply enhancing motivation by offering attractive rewards is often not enough to get them to fill high-status, in-demand jobs; and

3. There are many things about social stratification that appear to be dysfunctional to society. Examples include the frustration, desperation, and sense of hopelessness that poor people often experience, the increased risk of social problems such as crime and alcohol in poor neighborhoods, and the increased likelihood of destructive wars in societies where there is extreme social stratification.

The Conflict Perspective on Social Stratification

Marx's Theory

Karl Marx disagreed with the functionalist notion that the people who are in power deserve their privileged positions due to their special talents and abilities (Marx and Engels, 1967). Rather, Marx believed that in all capitalist societies, the people who are in power belong to a privileged social class that maintains their power through the control of scarce but valuable resources (e.g., oil, coal, steel) and the manipulation of social institutions (e.g., the judicial system and the educational system). This allows them to make huge profits through the exploitation of a second class of people who are powerless and dependent on them. Marx called these two social classes the **bourgeoisie** and the **proletariat**. The bourgeoisie own the means of production (e.g., oil companies, coal companies, steel companies, automobile companies) and gain wealth by exploiting the labor of the proletariat, who depend on wages received doing labor for the bourgeoisie. Because of the immense wealth and power that the bourgeoisie accumulate, they are able to influence laws, policy, and education in ways that maintain their power while keeping the proletariat dependent and powerless. Examples include limiting the power of labor unions or making them illegal, requiring coal miners or steel workers to buy their food and supplies on credit from a company-owned store (keeping them in a situation where they owe the company money), requiring them to live in company-owned houses (making them easy to evict if they stir up trouble), and paying minimal wages to ensure that their employees cannot afford to educate themselves or their children enough to escape dependence on company jobs.

Marx believed that the only way to halt this injustice is for the proletariat to unite, violently overthrow the capitalist system, and replace it with a classless society in which a government controlled by the people owns the means of production. Not only did he believe this conflict is necessary; he believed that it is inevitable. In Marx's view, the bourgeoisie and proletariat have diametrically opposing interests and are separated by a huge gulf of wealth, making it only a matter of time before the proletariat unite to overthrow their oppressors and improve their condition. Once the bourgeoisie minority is overthrown, Marx advocated that the capitalist system be replaced by a government-controlled system in which everybody's needs are met (Marx and Engels, 1967). Marx's ideas led to the communist revolutions in Russia, China, Cuba, and several other communist nations.

Critique of Marx's Theory

There are two major critiques of Marx's views on social stratification:

1. Marxism ignores an important central idea of the Davis-Moore theory, which is the notion that motivating people to do high-quality work may require a system of external rewards for "going the extra mile." The lack of such rewards may explain the apathy and low productivity that was typical of economic institutions in the Soviet Union (Nielsen, 2013; Osterfeld, 1986); and
2. The revolutions that Marx predicted have failed to happen in the advanced capitalist societies. Rather, they tend to happen only in poorer countries.

In regard to the second critique, Dahrendorf (1959) offers the following reasons for why Marxist revolutions haven't happened in advanced capitalist societies:

- The increasing overlap in the norms, behaviors, and roles between the capitalist social classes may interfere with strong identification with the working class. For example, many working-class people now own shares in industry stock, making them partial owners just like the bourgeoisie;
- There is a higher overall standard of living now than there was in Marx's time, creating a large middle class in advanced capitalist societies that is relatively content with the status quo;
- More organizations are devoted to the interests of workers in advanced capitalist societies now than in Marx's time; and
- There are more extensive legal protections in advanced capitalist societies now than in Marx's time.

Reflection Questions: Functionalist and Conflict Perspectives on Social Stratification

1. What do you think of Tumin's critique of the Davis-Moore theory? Can you add to his critique?
2. What do you think of the critique of Marx's theory? Can you add to this critique?
3. Do you agree more with the Davis-Moore theory or with Marx's theory? Why?

Social Stratification in the United Kingdom versus the Former Soviet Union

Despite the fact that social stratification doesn't always look exactly the same, it exists in all nations. To illustrate this point, consider the contrast between social stratification in the United Kingdom versus social stratification in the former Soviet Union.

Like the United States, Japan, Germany, and most other industrialized countries, the United Kingdom (a union of nations consisting of England, Scotland, Wales, and Northern Ireland) has a class system containing an upper class, a middle class, and a working class. While the working class and middle class are fairly equal in numbers, the upper class is tiny, making up about 1% of the population (Henslin, 2015). The British tend to be very class conscious (Aughey, 2012). Not only do they recognize differences in social class in the same ways that Americans do (e.g., by noticing what kind of car a person drives), they also can tell class difference by a person's accent, with "the Queen's English" being an indicator of upper-class affiliation and the London Cockney accent being an indicator of working-class affiliation. The upper class in the United Kingdom is also educated differently than the other two classes. While children of the middle and working classes tend to go to state-funded schools, the richest 5% (including the majority of British politicians) tend to go to exclusive private boarding schools and later to elite universities like Eton, Oxford, and Cambridge (Henslin, 2015; Neil, 2011).

In an attempt to create a classless society as advocated by Karl Marx, the Bolshevik Revolution of 1917 replaced the Russian Tsarist monarchy with a communist government that lasted 73 years (until 1990). Joined in 1922 by a group of other nearby nations (e.g., Estonia, Lithuania, Ukraine), this coalition of communist nations called itself the Soviet Union. While the Soviet leaders were proud of the fact that there was much less wealth inequality than in the United States and other capitalistic countries, there were huge disparities in privilege. Members of the Communist Party were able to go to better schools, obtain better housing, and obtain more desirable jobs. Furthermore, the higher up one's rank in the Communist Party, the greater the privileges (Matthews, 1978).

Social Stratification in the United States

As was previously mentioned, social class in the United States (as well as in other countries) is a product of one's wealth, power, and prestige. As we discuss American social stratification, we will revisit the concepts of wealth and power.

Wealth in America

As of 2014, the average (or *mean*) wealth in the United States was $301,000 per person, putting us in the fourth place behind Switzerland, Australia, and Norway (Luhby, 2014). If you are thinking "I thought my parents were doing pretty well, but they don't make anywhere near $301,000. Surely this must be a typo," then your suspicions are understandable. Even though this statistic is accurate, it is also very misleading. Simply stated, it is the result of increasingly high social stratification. Due to the increasingly high level of wealth disparity between social classes in the United States, the average salary of $301,000 is skewed high due to the presence of a small but extremely wealthy American superclass that is thriving economically, while the middle and working classes are actually losing ground.

While the United States hosts a very high percentage of the world's millionaires (42%, according to Luhby, 2014), most Americans do not belong to that superclass, and thus earn much more modest salaries. The *median* wealth in the United States in 2014, which represents the number at which 50% of Americans earn less and 50% earn more, and thus is a much better indicator of how the middle class is doing, was only $44,900 per adult. While this still makes the American middle class much wealthier than the vast majority other people worldwide, it only places the United States in the 19th place (below Canada, Japan, and much of Western Europe). Furthermore, the median wealth in the United States appears to be *decreasing* rather than increasing. For example, the median wealth of American families dropped nearly 40% between 2007 and 2010. Kenneth Thomas, a professor of political science at the University of St. Louis, suggests that possible reasons for the decline in the wealth of the American middle class (as reported by Luhby, 2014) are:

- the decline in the power of labor unions,
- the shifting of jobs overseas, and
- the increasing use of automated technology in the workplace.

Power in America

In the United States, individuals have the power to vote, and often (depending on the job they hold) their opinions are solicited regarding company policy and decisions. As such, Americans have a higher level of power than citizens of totalitarian dictatorships such as North Korea or Syria. However, sociologists Daniel Hellinger and Dennis Judd (1991) suggest that American citizens may not have as much power as they are inclined to believe they have. Calling this the **democratic façade**, Hellinger and Judd assert that despite our votes and participation in planning committees, the big decisions in the United States tend to reflect an ideology promoted by powerful elites to perpetuate their own agendas. The idea here is not so much that our votes don't count; rather, it's the notion that our votes have been manipulated as a result of having been presented with limited information and a skewed ideology that is likely to promote the agenda of the "powers that be."

C. Wright Mills (1956) coined the term **the power elite** to describe a small alliance of government, military, and corporate officials who control American wealth and policy. As evidence for the notion that wealth and power tend to coalesce in a special group of people with similar worldviews, Domhoff (1970, 1974, 2006) points out that members of the power elite tend to belong to the same private clubs, vacation at the same resorts, and even hire the same bands for parties. Furthermore, it is interesting to note that the majority of U.S. presidents have been white, male millionaires who come from "old money families" (Baltzell and Schneiderman, 1988).

Poverty in America

In the 1960s, the U.S. government began to define the poverty line as spending more than one-third of your total pre-tax cash income on minimum food necessities. The U.S. Census Bureau computes a minimal yearly food budget and multiplies that number by three. Anybody whose yearly income is less than this number is considered to be below the poverty line. Although this method has been criticized as an underestimate of poverty, the U.S. Census Bureau continues to use this formula for determining the poverty line, with periodic updates for the cost of minimum food necessities to account for inflation (Institute for Research on Poverty, 2016; Uchitelle, 2001).

In 2016, 14.0% of people in the United States lived below the poverty line, down from 14.7% in 2015 and 15.5% in 2014 (Hansen, 2017). For the past 150 years, the highest poverty rates have occurred in the South (Henslin, 2015), with Mississippi being the state with the highest percentage of people living in poverty, at 20.8% in 2016 (Hansen, 2017). Because whites are the largest race/ethnicity in the United States, poor whites outnumber poor people in all other racial/ethnic groups. However, percentage-wise, Native Americans, Latinos, and African Americans are more likely than whites to live in poverty. Furthermore, largely because women tend to earn less than men, women are more likely to be poor than men, especially if they are single or divorced (Henslin, 2015). This increased likelihood of women experiencing poverty than men (especially in low-income nations, but also in some high-income nations such as the United States) is referred to as the **feminization of poverty** (Pearce, 1978)

Reflection Questions: Social Stratification in the United States

1. Does the discrepancy between the 2014 mean wealth in the United States ($301,000) and the 2014 median wealth ($44,900) in the United States surprise you? Do you think things have improved for the American middle class since 2014, or do you think the trend toward decreased yearly wealth has continued?
2. In addition to the reasons provided by Kenneth Thomas (as cited in Luhby, 2014), can you think of any additional reasons for the decline in middle-class wealth in the United States? Do you agree or disagree with Thomas's reasons?
3. What is your opinion regarding Hellinger and Judd's (1991) notion of the *democratic facade*? Does it actually exist? Can you provide an example?
4. Do you believe that there is a power elite controlling American wealth and policy? Why or why not?

Global Stratification: A Comparison Between High-, Middle-, and Low-Income Nations

In the global stratification system, the 200-plus nations of the world are ranked in a hierarchy based on their access to the world's wealth, power, and prestige (Thompson and Hickey, 2007). Just as members of the upper class within the United States possess most of the American income, a handful of the world's most privileged nations control most of the world's wealth. In fact, global stratification is more unbalanced than social stratification within the United States. To fully grasp this point, consider the following comparisons between social stratification statistics in the United States and global stratification statistics:

- Whereas in the United States, the richest 1% of Americans control 38.6% of the nation's wealth (Egan, 2017), globally the richest 1% control 50.1% of all the world's wealth (Picchi, 2017).
- Whereas the poorest 20% of Americans own about 3% of the nation's wealth (Lenzner, 2013), globally the poorest 73% own only 2.4% of the world's wealth (Davies, Lluberas, and Shorrocks, 2016).

The remainder of this section will examine social stratification in high-income, middle-income, and low-income nations.

High-Income Nations

High-income nations have advanced industrial economies and high living standards (Thompson and Hickey, 2007). Examples include the United States, Canada, Israel, Japan, South Korea, Australia, Singapore, and most Western European countries. High-income nations receive a disproportionate share of the world's wealth and income. In 2016, the gross national income per capita of high-income nations was $41,150 per year (The World Bank Group, 2018a). Most of the people in these countries own cars and well-furnished homes or apartments. Containing about 16% of the world's population, even the poor in high-income nations live better and longer lives than average citizens in low-income nations (Henslin, 2015).

Middle-Income Nations

Middle-income nations have moderate wealth and living standards, and are usually newly industrialized (Thompson and Hickey, 2007). Examples include China, India, Mexico, Brazil, Columbia, Romania, Bulgaria, South Africa, and most of the nations that were once part of the Soviet Union. In 2016, the gross national income per capita of middle-income nations was $4891 per year (The World Bank Group, 2018c). Although people living in middle-income nations usually have necessities such as small homes or apartments and adequate food, late model cars and luxury appliances are less common. Containing about 16% of the world's population (Henslin, 2015), people in middle-income nations tend to live very modestly compared to most Americans.

Low-Income Nations

Low-income nations are poor and agrarian, and benefit the least from the global economy (Thompson and Hickey, 2007). Examples include Afghanistan, Haiti, North Korea, and many nations in sub-Saharan Africa (e.g., Ethiopia, Mozambique, Democratic Republic of the Congo). In 2016, the gross national income per capita of low-income nations was a meager $614 per year (The World Bank Group, 2018b). Most people in low-income countries are extremely poor. They typically have no access to indoor plumbing, trained teachers, or doctors. Containing about 68% of the world's population (Henslin, 2015), the *lifetime* incomes of most people in low-income nations are less than the *yearly* incomes of people in many high-income nations (Thompson and Hickey, 2007).

Many people in low-income nations experience **absolute poverty**, which is defined as lacking the basic necessities of life, such as food and safe water (Thompson and Hickey, 2007). About 3.1 million children die from starvation each year. About 17,000 children starved to death every day in 2013. The highest risk of a child dying before age five is in Africa, at a rate of 90 out of 1000 live births. This is seven times higher than the risk of dying before age five in Europe (World Hunger Education Service, 2016). In addition, it has been estimated that about 100 million children beg, steal, sell sex, or work for drug gangs to supplement the incomes of their families (Macionis, 2004).

Correlates of Global Poverty

Certain patterns have consistently been detected in nations with extreme poverty. John Macionis (2004) lists the following six things that seem to correlate with global poverty:

1. **Primitive technology:** For example, poorer cultures tend to rely on energy sources such as human muscles and beasts of burden rather than steam, oil, or nuclear power;
2. **High population growth:** The poorest countries in Africa and Asia tend to have the highest birth rates. For example, if the current population growth rate of 4.8% in Afghanistan remains constant (which, fortunately, is unlikely), its population will double every 14.5 years (Rosenberg, 2017);
3. **Resistance to change:** There is often much greater resistance to change and more emphasis on tradition in poorer countries;
4. **Very high social stratification:** The greatest discrepancy between the "richest rich" and the "poorest poor" is found in low-income nations;
5. **Gender inequality:** Because women tend to have very few rights and opportunities in the poorest countries, they are typically affected the most by poverty; and
6. **Colonialization:** Most low-income nations were once colonies of wealthier, more powerful Western European nations such as France, Spain, and England.

Theories of Global Poverty

Dependency Theory: The Negative Impact of Colonialism

Dependency theory (Baran, 1957; Harrison, 1993; Prebisch, 1950; Singer, 1949; Singer, 1950) asserts that when rich industrialized nations invaded and colonized weaker nations in the 1500s through the early 1900s, they created a situation in which the "mother countries" profited while the colonies were exploited and kept poor. Because colonies were made dependent on their colonizers, they never had the power or opportunity to fully develop their economies.

Even though the age of colonization is over, with nearly all former colonies now independent nations, these countries sometimes still remain dependent on their former colonizers. Michael Harrington (1977) called this **neocolonialism**. Four factors related to the dependency of poor nations on rich nations in the neocolonialist system are:

1. **Defense dependence:** The leaders of poor countries often depend on the purchase of weapons from wealthier countries in order to maintain their power (Henslin, 2015). This not only creates increased monetary debt, but also a situation in which a regime's very existence is dependent on the goodwill of a more powerful nation (e.g., Syria's Bashir Assad's dependence on the support of his Russian ally, Vladimir Putin);
2. **Trade dependence:** Poor nations sell raw materials and foods cheaply to rich nations, where factories process them and they're sold. Therefore, most of the money goes to the richer "buyer nations," who sell the finished products at much higher prices while people in the "seller nations" remain poor (Thompson and Hickey, 2007). As a striking example, sometimes the tropical foods that we enjoy in the United States are grown and picked by people whose wages are so low that they cannot afford to eat any of it;
3. **Industrial dependence:** Poor nations often have to buy expensive technology from wealthy nations to grow their food exports or mine their mineral exports, thus adding to their debt (Thompson and Hickey, 2007); and

4. **Investment dependence:** The high debts that poor countries owe wealthy countries keep the poor countries dependent while contributing to their high inflation and economic stagnation (Thompson and Hickey, 2007).

Sometimes, a low-income country's citizens are dependent on a specific **multinational corporation**. This was the case in the 1940s and 1950s, when the U.S.-based United Fruit Company had great political influence on the conditions of the Guatemalan laborers in its employ (Schlesinger and Kinzer, 1982). After Jacobo Arbenz became president of Guatemala in 1951, he began to implement land reform laws that threatened the interests of the United Fruit Company. As a result, the company was able to convince leaders in the Eisenhower administration that Arbenz intended to turn Guatemala into a Soviet-dominated threat to the security of the Western Hemisphere (i.e., a second Cuba). Reacting against this supposed threat, the CIA orchestrated a coup against him, resulting in Arbenz's overthrow in 1954.

World System Theory

According to Immanuel Wallerstein (1974, 2004), and also as summarized by sociologist Frank Elwell (2013), industrialization led to three groups of nations: core nations, semiperiphery nations, and periphery nations. Core nations such as England, Germany, the United States, and Japan industrialized first, and have become rich and powerful as a result. Semiperiphery nations such as Mexico, Brazil, China, and India developed more slowly, but their economies are improving as they industrialize. While semiperiphery nations continue to be exploited by core nations for the cheap labor they provide, they have profited from expansion into manufacturing in areas that core nations no longer find profitable (e.g., textiles, toys and other gadgets, furniture that is typically sold cheaply at large American discount franchises). Periphery nations such Indonesia, Thailand, Pakistan, and almost all African nations remain relatively undeveloped and are sometimes exploited for cheap labor (e.g., "sweat shops").

The nations that belong to each of Wallerstein's categories have changed significantly over the centuries, as former periphery nations such as China and India have become current semiperiphery nations, and former semiperiphery nations such as the United States and Japan have become core nations. At the beginning of the age of capitalism and world trade in the 1500s (Wallerstein, 1974), the core nations were exclusively Western and Northern European countries (e.g., England, France, Holland); the semiperiphery nations included former world powers in decline such as Portugal, Spain, and Italy; and the periphery nations were Eastern European countries (especially Poland) and Latin American countries, which were exploited for cheap labor and raw materials. In addition, during this time there was a fourth category of nations that were excluded from the development of capitalism and world trade, and thus remained largely agrarian and isolated. 16-century Russia was an example of an excluded nation. As the world has become completely globalized, however, this fourth category has ceased to exist. Even countries that have isolated themselves from the United States, such as North Korea, trade with other nations (e.g., China).

The Culture of Poverty Theory

John Kenneth Galbraith (1979) asserted that impoverished nations are held back by their own cultures. Defining **culture of poverty** as a way of life that perpetuates poverty from one generation to the next, Galbraith argued that most of the world's poor people are farmers who work small plots of land. Producing barely enough food to survive, they fear risk. This causes them to stick with traditional ways of farming that they are familiar with, despite the fact that the traditional techniques are much less efficient than the more modern techniques. This resistance to change and modernization is also fueled by religious beliefs that encourage the poor to simply accept their situations. For example, the Dalit caste in India are sometimes taught that the reason for their lowly status is that they have done very bad things in a previous life and that they should therefore just accept that this is their just punishment and hope for reincarnation into a more desirable state in their next life (Henslin, 2015).

Reflection Questions: Global Poverty

1. Have you ever lived in or visited a middle-income nation? If so, what differences in the day-to-day existence of people seemed to be the most striking?
2. Have you ever lived in or visited a low-income nation? If so, what differences in the day-to-day existence of people seemed to be the most striking?
3. Which of the three theories of global poverty (dependency theory, world system theory, or culture of poverty theory) do you like best? Why?

References

Anderson, M. June 9, 2008a. The Clergy and the Nobility: The French Revolution. *Big Site of History: History of Civilization.* https://bigsiteofhistory.com/the-clergy-and-the-nobility-the-french-revolution/

Anderson, M. June 9, 2008b. The Third Estate: The French Revolution. *Big Site of History: History of Civilization.* https://bigsiteofhistory.com/the-third-estate-the-french-revolution/

Aughey, A. 2012. "Englishness as Class: A Re-examination." *Ethnicities* 12 (4): 394–408. http://citeseerx.ist.psu.edu/viewdoc/download?doi=10.1.1.864.8842&rep=rep1&type=pdf

Baltzell, E. D., and Schneiderman, H. G. 1988. "Social Class in the Oval Office." *Society* 25: 42–9.

Baran, P. A. 1957. *The Political Economy of Growth.* New York, NY: Monthly Review Press.

BBC News. July 20, 2017,. What Is India's Caste System? *BBC News.* http://www.bbc.com/news/world-asia-india-35650616

Cartwright, M. November 1, 2013. Slavery in the Roman World. *Ancient History Encyclopedia.* https://www.ancient.eu/article/629/slavery-in-the-roman-world/

Dahrendorf, R. 1959. *Class and Class Conflict in Industrial Society.* Stanford, CA: Stanford University Press.

Davies, J. B., Lluberas, R., and A. F. Shorrocks. 2016. The Global Wealth Report: 2016. *Credit Suisse Research Institute.* https://www.credit-suisse.com/corporate/en/articles/news-and-expertise/the-global-wealth-report-2016-201611.html

Davis, K., and W. E. Moore. 1945. "Some Principles of Stratification." *American Sociological Review* 10 (2): 242–9.

Domhoff, G. W. 1970. *The Higher Circles.* New York, NY: Random House.

Domhoff, G. W. 1974. *The Bohemian Grove and Other Retreats: A Study in Ruling Class Cohesiveness.* New York, NY: Harper and Row.

Domhoff, G. W. 2006. *Who Rules America? Power, Politics, and Social Change.* 5th edition. New York, NY: McGraw-Hill.

Egan, M. September 27, 2017. Record Inequality: The Top 1% Controls 38.6% of America's Wealth. *CNN Money.* http://money.cnn.com/2017/09/27/news/economy/inequality-record-top-1-percent-wealth/index.html

Elwell, F. W. 2013. Wallerstein's World-Systems Theory. http://www.faculty.rsu.edu/~felwell/Theorists/Essays/Wallerstein1.htm

Galbraith, J. K. 1979. *The Nature of Mass Poverty.* Cambridge, MA: Harvard University Press.

Hansen, C. September 26, 2017. States with the Highest Poverty Rate. *U.S. News and World Report.* https://www.usnews.com/news/best-states/slideshows/the-10-states-with-the-highest-poverty-rate

Harrington, M. 1977. *The Vast Majority: A Journey to the World's Poor.* New York, NY: Simon & Schuster.

Harrison, P. 1993. *Inside the Third World: The Anatomy of Poverty.* 3rd edition. London: Penguin Books.

Hellinger, D., D. R. Judd. 1991. *The Democratic Facade.* Pacific Grove, CA: Brooks/Cole.

Henslin, J. M. 2015. *Essentials of Sociology: A Down-to-Earth Approach.* 11th edition. Upper Saddle River, NJ: Pearson.

Hess, A. E. M., and T. C. Frohlich. November 23, 2014. Countries with the Most Enslaved People. *24/7 Wall St.* https://www.usatoday.com/story/money/2014/11/23/247-wall-st-countries-most-slaves/70033422/

Institute for Research on Poverty. 2018. *How is poverty measured in the United States?* Institute for Research on Poverty, Board of Regents of the University of Wisconsin System. https://www.irp.wisc.edu/resources/how-is-poverty-measured/

Jackson, A. August 5, 2017. Where America's 'First Kids' Went to College. *Business Insider.* http://www.businessinsider.com/where-kids-of-presidents-went-to-college-2017-8/#lynda-bird-johnson-robb-university-of-texas-at-austin-class-of-1966-1

Lenzner, R. April 19, 2013. The Wealthiest 20% Own 72%; The Poorest 20% Only 3%. *Forbes.* https://www.forbes.com/sites/robertlenzner/2013/04/19/the-growing-disparity-in-wealth-made-the-great-recession-worse-and-the-recovery-weaker-than-ever-before/#4c7f21244efc

Luhby, T. August 5, 2014. America's Middle Class: Poorer than You Think. *CNN Money.* http://money.cnn.com/2014/06/11/news/economy/middle-class-wealth/index.html

Macionis, J. J. 2004. *Sociology.* 10th edition. Upper Saddle River, NJ: Prentice Hall.

Marx, K., and F. Engels. 1967. *Communist Manifesto.* New York, NY: Pantheon.

Matthews, M. 1978. *Privilege in the Soviet Union: A Study of Elite Lifestyles Under Communism.* London: George Allen & Unwin.

Mills, C.W. 1956. *The Power Elite.* New York, NY: Oxford University Press.

Neil, A. January 26, 2011. Does a Narrow Social Elite Run the Country? *BBC News.* http://www.bbc.com/news/magazine-12282505

Nielsen, R. April 20, 2013. Why Did Communism Fail? [Blog post]. https://whistlinginthewind.org/2013/04/20/why-did-communism-fail-3-incentives/

Osterfeld, D. November 1, 1986. Socialism and Incentives. FEE: Foundation for Economic Education. https://fee.org/articles/socialism-and-incentives/

Pearce, D. 1978. "The Feminization of Poverty: Women, Work, and Welfare." *Urban and Social Change Review* 11 (1 and 2): 28–36.

Picchi, A. November 14, 2017. World's Richest 1% Control More than Half of All Wealth. *CBS News: Moneywatch.* https://www.cbsnews.com/news/richest-1-percent-control-more-than-half-of-all-wealth/

Polgreen, L. December 21, 2011. Scaling Caste Walls with Capitalism's Ladders in India. *New York Times.* http://www.nytimes.com/2011/12/22/world/asia/indias-boom-creates-openings-for-untouchables.html

Prebisch, R. 1950. The Economic Development of Latin America and Its Principal Problems (E/CN.12/89). Santiago: Economic Commission for Latin America and the Caribbean (ECLAC). http://archivo.cepal.org/pdfs/cdPrebisch/002.pdf

Rezaian, J. February 7, 2017. Slavery Is Still Alive in Mauritania. Can a New Court Ruling Help Change that? *The Washington Post: Today's Worldview.* https://www.washingtonpost.com/news/worldviews/wp/2018/02/07/slavery-is-still-alive-in-mauritania-can-a-new-court-ruling-help-change-that/?utm_term=.e00b84e0a4ee

Rosenberg, M. March 6, 2017. Population Growth Rates: Population Growth Rates and Doubling Time. *ThoughtCo.* https://www.thoughtco.com/population-growth-rates-1435469

Rothkopf, D. 2008. *Superclass: The Global Power Elite and the World They Are making.* New York, NY: Farrar, Straus, and Giroux.

Schlesinger, S. C., and S. Kinzer. 1982. *Bitter Fruit: The Untold Story of the American Coup in Guatemala.* New York, NY: Doubleday.

Singer, H. W. 1949. "Economic Progress in Underdeveloped Countries." *Social Research: An International Quarterly of Political and Social Science* 16 (1): 1–11.

Singer, H. W. 1950. "The Distribution of Gains Between Investing and Borrowing Countries." *American Economic Review* 40 (2): 473–85.

The World Bank Group. 2018a. High Income Data. *The World Bank.* https://data.worldbank.org/income-level/high-income

The World Bank Group. 2018b. Low Income Data. *The World Bank.* https://data.worldbank.org/income-level/low-income

The World Bank Group. 2018c. Middle Income Data. *The World Bank.* https://data.worldbank.org/income-level/middle-income

Thompson, W. E., and J. V. Hickey. 2007. *Society in Focus: An Introduction to Sociology.* 6th edition. Boston, MA: Allyn & Bacon.

Tumin, M. M. 1953. "Some Principles of Social Stratification: A Critical Analysis." *American Sociological Review* 18 (4): 387–94. http://web.ics.purdue.edu/~hoganr/SOC%20602/Spring%202014/Tumin%201953.pdf

Uchitelle, L. May 28, 2001. How to Define Poverty? Let Us Count the Ways. *New York Times.*

Wallerstein, I. 1974. *The Modern World System: Capitalist Agriculture and the Origins of the European World Economy in the Sixteenth Century.* New York, NY: Academic Press.

Wallerstein, I. 2004. *World Systems Analysis: An Introduction.* Durham, NC: Duke University Press.

Weber, M. 1947. *The Theory of Social and Economic Organization.* Translated by A. M. Henderson, and T. Parsons. Edited by T. Parsons. Glencoe, IL: Free Press.

Weber, M. 1968. *Economy and Society: An Outline of Interpretive Sociology.* Edited and translated by G. Roth, and C. Widdich. Berkeley, CA: University of California Press.

World Hunger Education Service. 2016. World Child Hunger Facts. *Hunger Notes.* https://www.worldhunger.org/world-child-hunger-facts/

6 Deviance

What Is Deviance?

For sociologists, **deviance** is the violation of social norms and the rules of society. Deviance can be looked at in terms of behaviors, beliefs, and attitudes either on a small-scale basis (individual case-by-case scenario) or on a large-scale basis (deviance in general). If you go to a restaurant and your friends order hamburgers and you get a burrito, on a small scale, you have deviated from the group. You don't always get something different than they do, but this time you did. Any pressure you might have felt to do what your friends did was minimal. Your act of deviance was not noticed much by others either. The greater importance a behavior has in relation to social order and group harmony, the more significant a deviant behavior or act becomes. This is especially the case in regard to social expectation and norms, viewing deviance from a larger scale. Police officers typically don't wear shorts and a t-shirt but a uniform indicating their social status. To wear shorts and a t-shirt would deviate from the norm for police officers. A student who stands on her desk during class is also deviating from the social expectations of a student. Social expectation ranges from when it is appropriate to hold a door open for someone to when it is (if ever) appropriate to kill another human being. **Conformity** is obedience to social norms and the rules of society. When you conform, you are acting "normal," or "like everyone else." Like deviance, conformity can be viewed on a small-scale basis and/or from the standpoint of social expectation. Conformity also includes abiding by the rules given in a context. Whether conformity is "good" or "bad" depends on "the eye of the beholder."

Solomon Asch: Asch Conformity Experiments

In 1951, Solomon Asch conducted a laboratory experiment where he took groups of five to seven male college students and assigned them the perceptual task of determining "which line is the same." Each student was to look at a card with a line on it and then look at another (answer) card with three possible matches of that same line labeled "A,", "B," and "C." One of the lines on the answer card was the same as that on the first card, and the other two lines were clearly longer or shorter. Each participant, after determining their answer choice, was to communicate aloud which line (on the answer card) matched the length of that on the first card. However, the ability to perceive "which line is the same" was not directly what Asch was looking to observe. All but one of the participants were really actors, and Asch's true intentions were concerned with how the one naïve participant would answer if the other (actor) participants were to give obvious wrong answers. The actors were informed of the "true" goal of the experiment before the naïve participant arrived to partake of the "which line is the same" study. The naïve subject was introduced to the experiment (along with the other participants present in the lab with him) as a line perception test—the other participants being instructed beforehand of the true goal of the experiment. Before the experiment, all actors were instructed in detail as to how they should respond to each trial (card presentation) of the experiment. On the first two trials, all actors gave the

From *Introduction to Sociology* by Jason Hollar and Todd Martin. Copyright © 2018 by Kendall Hunt Publishing Company. Reprinted by permission.

correct response, along with the naïve subject. In a few of the trials, different actors would give the correct response and on others, an incorrect response. In 12 of the 18 total trials, all of the actors gave the same incorrect response. The group was seated such that the real participant always responded last. Asch found that one-fourth of the real participants would not conform to the actors, 1 in 20 totally conformed to the other actors, and the remainder conformed to the others only some of the times.

Deviance and Social Order

Deviance and conformity are relative terms, meaning what is deviant to some is not necessarily deviant to others. An act or behavior in one context can be normal, or conformist, when the very same behavior can be deviant in another context. Cheering and applause is typical for ballgames and concerts, but not so typical for funerals. Typical dress for women of the 19th century in the west consisted of bonnets, corsets, and camisoles but this is not typical for women in the 21st century. Driving on the right side of the road is normal in the United States but is abnormal in the U.K and Japan. Some norms are esteemed to the point that a society is "built" around them, and society insists that everyone conform to them. A **crime** is the violation of a law. Individuals who commit crimes are punished based on the law. A state or society creates laws to establish social order. Other types of norms, such as folkways and mores, establish social order but on a more informal (less enforced) level than a law. A **law** is a formal social rule, established by custom and enforced by authorities. Sometimes a society's laws and the authorities that enforce them are collectively referred to as the law. Law defines and regulates conduct by prohibiting certain behavior on the one hand and affirming acceptable behavior on the other. Society defines what is right and wrong while levying penalties for wrongful behavior, which in turn is intended to regulate behavior. Crimes involve defined offenses against "the people," which is referred to the responsibility of "the state," even though there may be individual victims. **Social order** is the social arrangements that the people of a society have become accustomed to and base their lives upon.

For sociologists, deviance and conformity are categories of how people react to norms and are neutral terms. Sometimes an individual does not have to DO anything to violate "normality." Merely, looking a certain way or possessing a trait is enough to "stand out" in a crowd.

Symbolic Interactionism and Deviance

Symbolic Interactionists look to understand how certain behaviors and symbols that an individual displays guides how others react or interact with the individual. Symbolic Interactionists also try to understand how deviant individuals interpret different situations.

Labeling Theory and Stigma

Becker (1966) points out that it is not the act that makes something deviant but the reaction to it. This reaction is often employed through the use of labels. When an individual violates a norm or value that is held by the majority of the group, the violator is recognized as deviant and labeled accordingly. **Labeling theory** posits that an individual's self-identity and behavior is affected by society's (the surrounding group) use of classifications and categorizations pertaining to behavior and other characteristics. Society uses labels for the sake of social order. When an individual's behavior is perceived as threatening (or confirming) the social order, labels are used by society to identify how that individual relates to the norm. Being labeled a "Nobel Prize winner," a "proud parent," or an "athlete" categorizes how an individual relates to the rest of the population concerning social norms. Being labeled a "drug addict" or a "felon" also has meanings to the rest of society but tend to carry a negative stigma. A **stigma** is an attribute, behavior, or reputation that makes an individual abnormal, as is determined based on cultural norms, and results in social disgrace to some degree for the individual. Goffman (1963) referred to stigma as the process of being rejected and denied a normal identity due to some violation of normalcy. A stigma can arise due to a violation of norms concerning appearance, and/or behavior, and/or both.

Differential Association Theory

When a community is disorganized with reference to crime, for instance, one or more groups within that community are organized for crime and one or more groups within the community are organized against crime (Sutherland, 1945).

Sociologists emphasize that our behavior is heavily based on the experiences we have with the groups we associate. Different groups learn different attitudes and behaviors concerning deviance and conformity. Sutherland (1924, 1947) proposed **differential association theory,** a learning theory of deviance, where the individual interacts with a group and uses this interaction as the basis of how to interpret deviation from or conformity to society's norms. Individuals learn how to commit criminal acts as well as motives, drives, and attitudes concerning those criminal acts. A person becomes a criminal because the individual is exposed to more definitions favorable to violation of the law than to definitions favorable to conforming to the law.

For example, let's say a guy named Joe sells meth to make money to pay his rent and buy groceries. Selling drugs like meth is against the law, but Joe finds selling meth is easier than obtaining a "normal" or acceptable job that is legal. Selling drugs brings in more money than most jobs that Joe can get, being a convicted felon. Moreover, selling drugs is pretty common in Joe's neighborhood; most people in the neighborhood do it or know someone who does. In an unusual way, selling illegal substances has become the "norm" in Joe's neighborhood though not in the rest of society. In Joe's neighborhood, he would be deviant (or abnormal) if he didn't sell illegal substances (or engage in other criminal behaviors), and by selling meth he is actually conforming to his neighborhood's norms. True, Joe's neighborhood is deviant to most other neighborhoods in the country (and considered a "bad" neighborhood to them), but within Joe's neighborhood the norms have changed somewhat. Why does this happen when selling drugs is against the law? According to differential association theory, Joe *learned* (perhaps at a young age) that the best way to "make a living" in his neighborhood is engaging in selling illegal substances, despite the fact it is illegal. Joes uses his interaction with the rest of the people in his neighborhood as the basis of how to interpret deviation from the rules/laws of the greater society. He's seen it done (selling meth), has known people who do it and taught him how to do it "effectively," and therefore participates in the same behavior as a way to make money. To Joe, this is how you survive in his neighborhood, despite the consequences from being caught by the authorities. Joe has also been exposed to more definitions favorable to violation of the law than to definitions favorable to conforming to the law. You could say that it is normal to see the law in a negative light in Joe's neighborhood. Definitions of the authorities, for those in Joe's neighborhood, might support ideas that the authorities don't care about them or are against them and just want to make it impossible for them to "make a living." Those definitions might even go as far as blaming the authorities for making Joe's neighborhood as it is. To add to that, the cultural goals that appeal to most other neighborhoods are considered "pipe dreams" and unrealistic in Joe's neighborhood. Joe might believe, like most people in his neighborhood, going to college or getting a high school diploma is a fairytale that only happens for those in better-off neighborhoods. To him, to aspire to those ambitions is similar to believing in Santa Claus or the tooth fairy.

Control Theory

Control theory proposes that throughout the process of socialization we develop self-control and reduce our desire to indulge in antisocial behavior. Control theory explains why people conform instead of deviate to social expectations and the law. Reckless (1961) developed a version of control theory, known as containment theory, where he elaborated that people have inner (psychological) and outer (social) containments that help them refrain from antisocial behavior. The inner control or containment refers to one's self image ("am I the type of person who breaks the law?"). The outer containment refers to one's social influences ("my family and friends might ostracize me if they see me as a law breaker"). Reckless believed that inner containment was more influential than outer controls. Hirschi (1969) attempted to describe lawful, conformist behavior by emphasizing that the stronger our attachments to society, the more effective our inner controls are going to be. Hirschi proposed that we learn self-control (inner control) from *attachments* (our respect for those who uphold norms), *commitments* (having a status in society you don't want to lose by breaking a norm), *involvements* (our participation in approved activities), and *beliefs* (our convictions about right and wrong).

Structural Functionalism and Deviance

Deviance as Functional

> Imagine a society of saints, a perfect cloister of exemplary individuals. Crimes or deviance, properly so-called, will there be unknown; but faults, which appear venial to the layman, will there create the same scandal that the ordinary offense does in ordinary consciousnesses. If then, this society has the power to judge and punish, it will define these acts as criminal (or deviant) and will treat them as such Durkheim (1895/1982).

Durkheim suggested that punishing deviance affirms the value of specific norms to a society, and therefore creates social unity. For instance, if wearing clothes designed with polka dots was for some reason repulsive to a society, and the punishment for doing so was death, then the punishment would create a sense of brevity concerning polka dots for everyday citizens. Going as far as formally punishing citizens for violating a norm (as opposed to just looking at them weird or laughing at them) would help affirm the seriousness of keeping the norm and encourage law-abiding conformists (most people) to adhere to it. Conversely, deviance can lead to social change if the deviance causes enough people to reevaluate the accepted norms. Those who initiate social change challenge the existing state of affairs and start out deviant concerning the norm. They think "outside the box" and their unconventional ways or beliefs begin to be considered or accepted by others until eventually what was deviant becomes the new norm. What was considered deviant is now considered a better way to help society function (or fulfill its functions). Here we see deviance (and the classification of deviance) as a functional contributor to the development of society.

Strain Theory

> The self-fulfilling prophecy is, in the beginning, a false definition of the situation evoking a new behaviour which makes the original false conception come "true." This specious validity of the self-fulfilling prophecy perpetuates a reign of error. For the prophet will cite the actual course of events as proof that he was right from the very beginning. (Merton, 1948)

Robert Merton describes how the general perceptions of prejudices of some social groups toward other social groups can determine reality for all involved. If social group X has determined that social group Y is criminal in most respects, then some members, even most members, of social group Y may accept that definition of where they fit in society as true. Therefore, social group Y is "living up to" the expectations of social group X by accepting social group X's definition of them. They become the criminals they were expected to be (instead of trying to contribute to society in other ways) by internalizing the labels applied to them by social group X. Robert Merton (1938) also proposed **strain theory** to explain crime by stating that individuals feel societal pressure to achieve societal goals (like success and monetary achievement), but do not have sufficient access to the approved means of reaching those goals. When an individual cannot accomplish societal goals by approved means, she feels alienated and reacts in a deviant manner. This often leads individuals to obtain culturally approved goals through crime. However, not all people resort to crime, but still often resort to deviance. Merton categorized deviance and conformity based on how people react to obtaining societal goals.

(The following, by means of example, is based on a society that socializes its members to pursue the cultural goals of achieving success -success defined as obtaining a large amount of material gain- by working a legal/legitimate job and/or by going to college to obtain a legal/legitimate job.)

1. Conformity-societal goals are accepted; the means to obtain those goals are accepted in this situation, we have a description of people who follow the rules to pursue cultural goals. The "conformist" desires success and works a job or goes to college to increase her chances of achieving success.
2. Innovation-societal goals are accepted; unconventional and socially unapproved means (crime and "cheating the system") are substituted for traditional and socially acceptable means. The "innovator," like the conformist, desires success. The innovator does not follow the rules to obtain this success, like working a legitimate job or going to college to get a better job. Instead, she resorts to fraudulent investment operations to make more money. Having a lot of money will get her recognized as a success in her society.
3. Ritualism-societal goals are rejected; adhere to socially accepted means to obtaining the goals. The "ritualist" will not pursue the cultural goal of success (or will "settle" for not obtaining it) by societal definitions but will still work a legitimate job and/or go to college despite never obtaining "success" (as defined by society).
4. Retreatism-reject societal goals; reject the means to get goals. The "retreatist" doesn't participate much, but looks to escape society. They don't look to be successful, neither do they adhere to the means to do so. Instead, retreatists might be drug addicts or homeless or those who isolate themselves from society.
5. Rebellion-reject societal goals; reject the means to get goals. The "rebel" looks to redefine what is considered "success" or if "success" is even what people should be looking for. They also look to replace the accepted societal means (working a legitimate job or going to college) to obtain those goals. The rebel refuses to go along with societal ideals.

The Conflict Perspective

C. Wright Mills (1959) was critical of the sociology that was conducted "in his day" because it was all too eager to rely on either theory (Grand theory) or statistical data (abstract empiricism) to substantiate claims concerning the condition and nature of people. Essentially, he believed that politics and history had a lot of influence on the type of research that was being conducted and even the results that many social scientists were claiming. He believed that researchers could formulate results that would confirm their initial bias, even when using statistical analysis and science (the methods). One must take into account their own bias (and biography) when conducting any type of research, considering also the historical (and political) developments that might contribute. "Scientific research" can be used to create and confirm categories (labels) that do not accurately address the personal troubles that individuals in a social setting are experiencing, but instead are merely stereotypes presented as rational generalizations. This is what Mills observed when he wrote *The Sociological Imagination*.

This line of thought is echoed by sociologists and feminists such as Barbara Ehrenreich and Deirdre English (1978) who argued that medical experts (exclusively men) during the 19th and early 20th centuries attributed most problems and issues that women experienced to menstruation and pregnancy. Of course, the medical experts of the day suggested these diagnoses were scientific. In this case, science helped to create and confirm stereotypes concerning women. This historical and patriarchal practice of science and medicine helped constrain women, in general, to a very limited work (and domestic) social sphere, one that was ridiculed and protested during the women's movement of the late 1960s.

Medicalization of Deviance

The **medicalization of deviance** is a term used to describe how human problems, behavior, and conditions are diagnosed and treated as entirely medical conditions. A deviation that is social in nature is redefined or understood as having biological premises. This perception is based on the biomedical model of disease. Do all forms of social deviance have a biological basis? Is there a drug or drugs that can make someone "normal," or at least closer to "normal" whatever the problem? Conflict theorists propose that the elites, through the criminal justice system and even through institutions like health care, decide what is "normal" and deviant for society. Those who suggest that the medicalization of deviance has become a problem of vast proportions in our technological age do not question medical knowledge itself, but the application of such knowledge—is medicine the best solution to all our problems? According to psychiatrist and academic Thomas Szasz (2007), a "genuine" disease is one that entails an objectively identifiable disturbance in healthy cell function, tissue, or organs. But with medicalization (of deviance), diseases are constructed and projected onto patients specifically so as to justify treatments and medicines, regardless if a biological condition can be identified. Many are concerned about the relationship that pharmaceutical companies have with the medical profession, especially psychiatry. Thomas Szasz suggested that medical ethics, particularly "coercive psychiatric practices," should be challenged not only to avoid the misdiagnosis and labeling of individuals, but also to avoid abuses within (and by) the medical profession. Medicine may change or alleviate the symptoms, but is it addressing (and correcting) a biological condition (if there is one)? Is classifying conditions like drug addiction a "disease" an accurate assessment? Would the wealthy elites who stand to profit from the medicalization of deviance take advantage of the poorer classes just to make a profit? Conflict theorists would suggest so.

Pyrrhic Defeat Theory

Pyrrhic defeat theory is formed by Jeffrey Reiman (1979), who states that the criminal justice system does not function to eliminate or fight crime. Instead, the wealthy and powerful control the criminal justice system to create a specific image of crime, to the rest of society, that crime is a product of the poor. This way, public discontent and opposition is directed toward the poor and not toward the wealthy and powerful. The message sent out by the wealthy is that the poor are the problem and they need to be fixed or avoided. The criminal justice system serves as a vehicle to support this notion in that laws are written, judges sentence criminals, and police/prosecutors discern and arrest in a manner where the poor represent the larger, more imminent threat to society. The criminal justice statistics will then consequently reflect this process. In this theory, the poor are used as a scapegoat. A **scapegoat** in sociology is a group that is blamed for a social condition or problem that they are unrelated to or unlikely responsible for.

References

Asch, S. E. 1951. Effects of group pressure on the modification and distortion of judgments. In *Groups, Leadership and Men*. Edited by H. Guetzkow, 177–90. Pittsburgh, PA: Carnegie Press.

Becker, H. S. 1966. *Outsiders: Studies in the Sociology of Deviance*. New York, NY. Free Press.

Durkheim, E. 1982/1895. *Rules of Sociological Method*. New York, NY: The Free Press.

Ehrenreich, B., and D. English. 1978. *For Her Own Good: 150 Years of the Experts' Advice to Women*. Garden City, NY: Anchor Press.

Goffman, E. 1963. *Stigma: Notes on the Management of Spoiled Identity*. New York, NY: Touchstone Publishers.

Hirschi, T. 1969. *Causes of Delinquency*. Berkeley, CA: University of California Press.

Merton, R. 1938. "Social Structure and Anomie." *American Sociological Review* 3 (5): 672–82.

Merton, R. K. 1948. "The Self Fulfilling Prophecy." *Antioch Review* 8 (2): 506–7.

Mills, C. W. 1959/2000. *The Sociological Imagination*. New York, NY: Oxford University.

Reckless, W. C. December, 1961. "A New Theory of Deliquency and Crime." *Federal Probation* 25 (4): 42–6.

Reiman, J. 1979. Criminal justice through the looking glass. In *The Rich Get Richer and the Poor Get Prison*. New York, NY: John Wiley & Sons.

Sutherland, E. H. 1924. *Criminology*. Philadelphia, PA: Lippincott.

Sutherland, E. H. 1945. "Social Pathology." *American Journal of Sociology* 50 (6): 431.

Sutherland, E. H. 1947. *Principles of Criminology*. 4th edition. Philadelphia, PA: Lippincott.

Szasz, T. S. 2007. *Medicalization of Everyday Life: Selected Essays*. Syracuse, NY: Syracuse University Press.

7 Family and Gender

Learning Objectives

7.1 Explain the concept and social construction of family and gender

7.2 Examine family and gender through sociological paradigms

7.3 Describe how family and gender have undergone a continuous change in meaning over time

7.4 Identify how family and gender are key agents in the process of socialization

All in the Family

Family is the primary agent of socialization; the starting point for sociologists in examining how people learn and participate in a society. Before we start to examine how vital the family is to society, we must first identify what a family is. A *family*, in its most basic form, is two or more individuals who live together and legally or normatively have a recognized relationship. Family is not simply a heterogeneous couple who have been legally married and have birthed their own children. A family can encompass many types of relationships such as a homosexual couple who are either legally married or who participate in a common-law marriage. It can involve children, either birthed by the couple, adopted, or a relative such as a grandmother raising her grandchildren. Since sociologists examine groups of people and trends, we look at how family and marriage change with the social landscape. Based on these changes, we start to reexamine what family looks like, and more importantly, the function family serves in society.

Throughout the history of the United States and Canada, family has evolved, and primarily it has done so because the concept of *marriage* has evolved. Marriage is seen as a culturally normative relationship between two individuals. Marriage, despite the romantic feelings associated with it, is a legal process. When a couple decides to get married, they will register

Family: Two or more individuals who identify as being related to one another; not dependent upon blood, marriage, or adoption ties.

Marriage: It is considered a permanent social and legal contract and relationship between two people that is based on mutual rights and obligations among the spouses.

From *Exploring Sociology* by Mariah Jade Zimpfer. Copyright © 2018 by Kendall Hunt Publishing Company. Reprinted by permission.

with the county in which they reside and apply for a marriage certificate. This is because marriage has evolved to include legal sanctions such as individuals are not allowed to marry family members or individuals currently married to someone else. These laws reflect the norms of the community, such as it is taboo to marry someone you are related to, and to marry multiple people is culturally not accepted because polygamy and polyandry no longer legally exist in North America. Marriage used to be a process of necessity. If you have ever been to a wedding, typically the father of the bride will walk the bride down the aisle and the minister will ask, "who gives this woman away?" This is a cultural holdover from when women had dowries and did not have rights. Therefore, the father had to legally and culturally claim that he was giving up his rights over her and giving her to another man who would hold her rights. In today's wedding ceremonies, this act is traditional rather than culturally pertinent. Additionally, there was a point in our history in which antimiscegenation laws existed—these prohibited interracial relationships. It wasn't until 1967 with the Loving v. Virginia case were these laws considered unconstitutional.

Antimiscegenation Laws: Laws that enforce racial segregation at the level of marriage and intimate relationships by criminalizing interracial marriage.

Loving v. Virginia: A landmark civil rights decision of the US Supreme Court, which invalidated laws prohibiting interracial marriage.

Families: Theoretical Perspectives

Functionalist Perspective

When we discuss families, not only do we examine who constitutes a family, but also as important is what function does the family serve. For sociologists, the primary function of family is to care for all members within the family, most notably the children. There are legal and social definitions regarding expectations of what is appropriate care for minors—individuals under the age of 18. However, sociologists also examine the role of family regarding the socialization process. The family is where children first learn about the world, expectations of society, the norms and values within that society, and so forth. It is also within the family that children learn about culture, religion, education, and other important social institutions.

It is also within the family institution that we start to see individuals displaying different functions. For example, Parsons (1954) claimed that men and women perform different functions with the family. For him, women were seen as being expressive and men were seen as being instrumental; this resulted in what he termed as a "factory of personalities." Expressive meant that women were seen as nurturing, maternal, emotive, and that their sphere of dominance was within the home. Instrumental meant that men were seen as being teachers of aggression, working and earning money, and their sphere of dominance was outside of the home. Obviously, critics within the twenty-first century disagree with this for several reasons. One, Parsons theory is outdated merely on the fact that the composition of families has drastically changed. No longer is a family solely a heterogeneous coupling, but it is comprised of multiple relatives, homogenous couples, and single-parent households. Also, the demand for dual-income families became a necessity and therefore, women could no longer remain primarily within the household. Lastly, we currently see a rising trend of men staying home to take care of the children while women work.

Feminist Perspective

The feminist perspective is a category within the conflict perspective. Therefore, we should keep in mind the basic tenet of conflict theory in that conflict exists because of unequal distribution of power. Feminists examine the family as a site for both positive and negative aspects of power distribution. Until the 1980s, when we saw more women entering the workforce, families were seen as being heterosexual with the man working and the women taking care of the house. However, as previously mentioned, this time period also urged families to become dual-income earners in order to survive economically—and also more women were entering college in the 1970s—so the "typical" family was changing. With this change, brought conversations regarding the differing of role expectations. In 1982, Jessie Bernard wrote *The Future of Marriage* in which she explained that how we understand marriage was still, at this time, reminiscent of prior decades. She claimed that in

a heterosexual marriage, both partners experience a different kind of marriage—termed as "his" and "her" marriage. For him, his marriage is one in which he defines himself by what he can bring to the table, how he can assert his independence, show his machismo, and excel in his job. Her marriage is one which she seeks to define herself through the institution of marriage by showing her social capital of being married, having children, and how she keeps her house presentable as a private sphere of the relationship. This type of marriage is one in which feminist argue that there is an unequal distribution of power. Feminists would also argue that this concept does not include homosexual marriages, or families that constitute other relatives or single-parent households.

Families: Evolution of an Institution

As has been discussed throughout this chapter so far, families have changed throughout the years. With the passage of the **Marriage in Equality Act** (2011) the norm is switching from strictly heterosexual unions. According to the American Psychological Association (http://www.apa.org/topics/divorce/), 40%–50% of individuals will divorce in the United States. Despite this statistic, children are still growing up in two-parent households, 69% to be exact (census—https://www.census.gov/library/visualizations/2016/comm/cb16-192_living_arrangements.html)

So while families are changing, they're evolving to encompass a plethora of meanings for "family." Therefore, as a society, we are moving more toward being open with what family looks like and realizing that in many families—no matter the composition—individuals take on multiple roles.

Marriage in Equality Act: A 2011 New York State law that allows gender-neutral marriages for both same- and opposite-sex couples.

Social Class and Families

Social class and economics play a significant role in how families function and how people raise their children. Lareau (2002) indicated that social class impacts how children are raised because there are expectations of each class. For example, parents in poorer neighborhoods tend to raise their children to obey authority, rather than question it because the assumption is that the child will enter the workforce rather than go to college when the time is appropriate. Children whose parents are in the upper class are taught to be creative and question authority because the assumption is that they will earn several degrees and lead companies. These assumptions of class are not only found within the family and ways in which children are raised, but it is further indoctrinated when children go to school.

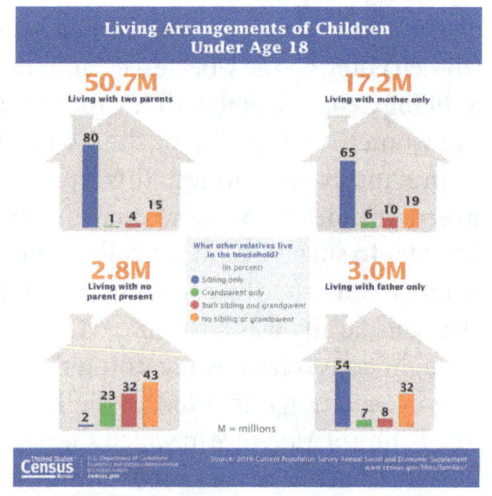

Gender

Gender is discussed alongside family because **gender roles** are first learned within the family. Gender is different from **sex** in that sex refers to anatomical components, and gender is a social construct. Gender tends to encompass norms, values, and behavioral characteristics associated with male or female; however, if they are not mutually exclusive. Because of this, sociologists tend to consider gender to be a fluid

Gender: Behavioral characteristics that are different between male and female based on cultural norms.

Gender Roles: Attitudes and behaviors which are considered "masculine" or "feminine" within a certain culture.

construct which changes across a person's lifetime and has no bearing on their sexuality or sex. Concepts such as masculinity and femininity refer to gender and can be used to describe both men and women equally. Currently, there are conversations around the concept of pronouns. Some people identify outside of heteronormative pronouns "he" and "she." Rather, there is a movement to include more gender inclusive pronouns such as: "zie," "sie," "ey," "ve," "tey," and "e" (https://uwm.edu/lgbtrc/support/gender-pronouns/). Many of these "new" pronouns are not new, but rather come from old English; it is actually "he" and "she" that are new pronouns. By engaging in conversations with how individuals want to be identified, we are giving people agency and authority over their identity. Additionally, we are establishing a dialogue for other concerns regarding gender. Gender is a fluid concept and one that changes in every situation, or at least, that is what West and Zimmerman (1987) concluded in their seminal article *Doing Gender*. "Doing gender" is based on the dramaturgical concept that we size up our situation and audience and then display a role that is fitting for the situation. Each encounter that someone has daily will change depending on how they see gender in the situation. For example, a woman who sees herself as feminine might be more nurturing and "motherlike" at home while getting the kids ready for school. At work, she might adopt a more strong "masculine" take-charge kind of role when she heading into a board meeting.

Sex: Refers to anatomical components, and gender is a social construct.

Gender and Family

Gender is found in all sociological institutions, but as noted earlier, the family plays a significant role in how individuals understand and develop their gender identity. Parents show gender socialization toward their children before they're born. Gender reveal parties, painting a nursery, choosing clothes and toys for the baby are mechanisms that we start to categorize individuals into a certain gender. Furthering this, the activities that parents engage their children in, such as sports or dance, are other methods that further this process of gender. Currently, some parents are trying to move away from this binary discussion of gender, but other institutions such as toy manufacturers do not make it easy. Additionally, the way parents talk about topics with their children, how they model their behavior in front of their children, can show gender without knowing it. For example, think back to when you were a child, which parent was responsible for which activities in the household? Which parent talked to you about puberty, school, dating, and work? We don't normally think of these episodes in our life until we are adults and we are about to get married or raise children of our own. But even from a young age, we were being socialized toward gender.

Gender and Peers

Once we start playing with other children and making friends, then our peers further reinforce our notions of gender. Girls and boys behave differently within their groups, and studies have indicated that boys are more harsh in reinforcing, or "policing" their peers (Martin and Fabes 2001; Aina and Cameron 2011). Boys tend to stigmatize and "punish" physically other boys who behave too feminine. Boys will call each other gay, queer, a fag, and a girl, if they are not behaving in a masculine way. This has led to the phenomenon known as **hegemonic masculinity**. Hegemonic masculinity refers to how men should behave—should be the operative word—and the consequences of trying to fit into such a rigid mold. If your professor were to ask you to make a list of male traits, you might write something to the effect of tough, plays sports, doesn't cry, doesn't show emotion, strong, and so forth. Hegemonic masculinity is the result of boys trying to fit into this category and therefore not engaging in dialogues that include boys having emotions, or boys not being good at sports, or perhaps boys as nurses.

Hegemonic Masculinity: A concept which reinforces strict heteronormative rules for masculine behavior.

Girls also reinforce gender stereotypes as well when they play. If a girl is too tough or prefers sports and doesn't engage fully in emotive or nurturing play, then other girls will criticize her, perhaps call her a tomboy. Studies have indicated that girls tend to gather in smaller groups, whereas boys in larger—similar to a sports team—and girls tend to imitate play (Richards 2012; Thorne 1993). For example, have you ever played or seen your younger sister playing the game house? Usually this involves a girl being the mother, a boy being the father, and some amount of children. The girl will unquestionably take on the role of mother and the stereotypical roles that come along with that such as cleaning the house, cooking the meals, and taking care of the children.

Gender and Media

Media is another institution in which we see how gender is represented. Often, the media is criticized for its unfair representation of women; but arguably, there are numerous instances where it doesn't represent men, or other gender identities well either. We can easily criticize models, fashion magazines, and billboards for the unfair and inadequate representation of women; but what about men? Men also do not get appropriate representation as well. Think for a minute when

you see men advertising cologne, sports gear, or clothes they are all athletic, tend to be either black or white, and young. What about other races and ethnicities being represented as well as different ages and body types? There are some changes that are happening in the media, but they are slow to appear. During Super Bowl LI (2017), they aired a Mister Clean commercial in which there was erotic music playing and Mister Clean was seductively dancing as he was cleaning, and the woman was just swooning. Then, Mister Clean turned into her husband. Other commercials have started to show men helping out with the kids by doing their hair or making breakfast. During a 2017 Valentine's Day commercial for a national retailer, it showed two women getting married. These are small moments on the television, but they open a dialogue to have larger conversations.

Gender and Sociological Theories

Classical Approaches

In the early days of the discipline, women did not have a place. The classic theorists such as Marx, Durkheim, and Weber would not have fully considered women's issues worth discussing. Women were seen as naturally inferior to men and their place was already decided in the home, not in the rest of society. Very few women were heard in the early years of the discipline. Charlotte Perkins Gillman was one of the few who made herself known. She coined the term sexuoeconomic relationship to describe the heterosexual relationship that women and men engage in—both wanting something from the other, and both understanding the woman had to rely upon the husband. At the time, this concept was monumental in understanding the lack of agency and position that women had in society. However, as time grew on, people began to criticize the concept because it fails to recognize nonheteronormative relationships.

> **Sexuoeconomic Relationship:** Concept which claims that in heterosexual relationships, men and women benefit from their spouse socially.

Feminism: A Contemporary Take on Gender

Feminism is the belief in gender equality. It is not the belief that women are better than men, this is reminiscent of sexism. Feminism encompasses social equality for all genders, not just men and

women. Feminism emerged in the United States during the Abolitionist Movement in the late 1840s. Elizabeth Cady Stanton and Lucretia Mott met in Seneca Falls, New York to set in motion the movement for women's rights. Eighty years later, women were given the right to vote when the nineteenth Amendment was passed. Since then, feminism has gone through many waves. In the 1960s, we see the second wave of feminism emerge after the seminal book by Betty Friedan (1963) *The Feminine Mystique*. Women during this time were rallying for equal opportunity, not unlike those in the 1800s. But since they came after the amendment passing, they were unlikely to truly understand the great strides and struggles that those former women went through. So, the second wave of feminism was a rebirth of similar issues.

Liberal feminism echoed the work of Friedan and concentrated on the imperfections of institutions, rather than individuals. Liberal feminists believe that in order for equality to exist then equality must first be present in the institutions. If you recall some of the topics discussed earlier in this chapter, this would look like equality in the home, in the classroom, and in the marriage. Socialist feminism concentrates on the divisions that are products of a capitalist market. Since women have not traditionally been the owners of the means of operation, they are therefore inherently inferior to men who are the owners of the means of operation. Radical feminism suggests that women's inequality is at the root of all inequality. They focus on inequality in religion, education, employment, the family, and all other aspects of society. Radical feminists encourage changing society's values and norms because they stem from patriarchy; and if these aren't changed, then women might accept them as normal. Multicultural feminism focuses on feminism regardless of age, race, gender, class, or nationality. Individuals who identify as multicultural feminism tend to start or create global networks and initiatives.

Feminism: Belief that social equality should exist between the sexes.

Sexism: Belief that one sex is inherently superior to the other.

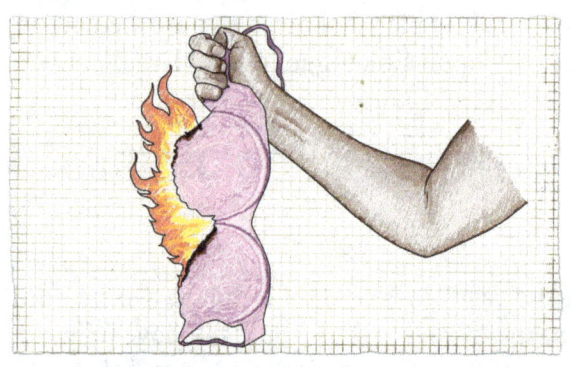

Liberal Feminism: Belief that women's inequality is a result of unequal institutions.

Socialist Feminism: Belief that women's inequality is rooted in all other forms of inequality and is the product of economic inequality found in capitalism.

Radical Feminism: Belief that women's inequality is at the root of all other equalities and to be equal, society must radically change.

Multicultural Feminism: Belief that inequality must end and be achieved for all women regardless of age, race, ethnicity, class, nationality, sexual orientation, or physical ability.

Conclusion

Family is the primary agent of socialization according to sociologists. It is within this institution that we start to learn about society and see our place within it. Our caregivers and other individuals who comprise our family teach us about society, religion, education, employment; but they also teach us about gender, roles associated with gender, and how we start to develop a dialogue about gender. Critics claim that gender is not in every situation we find ourselves in; but studies are quick to dispel that. In some instances in the twenty-first century, we are establishing new and forward thinking dialogues about gender; in other instances, such as gender reveal parties, we are not. This constant reflexive process that we engage with gender is also one that we find ourselves engaging with family. Both institutions are evolving, new conversations are emerging which focus on "what does family look like" and "how do we 'do' gender?" While these institutions seem separate, they are very much intertwined and shape our sense of the social world.

Activity

Watch the following video http://: https://www.youtube.com/watch?v=kLb5XSdLmAI and connect what you see in the video to some of the discussions in this chapter?

8 Race and Ethnicity

Race, Ethnicity, and Minority Groups

Race

Race can be defined as "a group whose inherited physical characteristics distinguish it from other groups" (Henslin, 2015, p. 253). There is great variety in the physical characteristics of humans. Skin color can range from a pale pinkish-white to a dark brown, with some people having yellowish or reddish hues. Hair can be straight, kinky, brown, blonde, reddish, or black. Eyes can be blue, brown, greenish, or amber.

However, despite the variety in the physical characteristics of humans, the notion that there are a fixed number of races that everybody agrees upon is a myth. Anthropologist Ashley Montagu (1942, 1964) pointed out that some scientists have classified humans into only two races, while others have claimed that there are up to 2000 races. Montagu's personal belief was that there are three racial categories into which people are often classified (Negroid, Caucasoid, and Mongoloid), with about 40 racial subgroups within these general categories (Montagu, 1951). Each subgroup has distinct physical differences. For example, although both fall within the Negroid category, the Oceanic people of Papua New Guinea look significantly different from the Bushman-Hottentot people of the Kalahari Desert in southern Africa. In another example, native Japanese people and Inuit in Alaska and Northern Canada look significantly different even though both are often classified as Mongoloid.

Another myth about race is the notion that there are separate "pure races." Even if there once were pure races, most people alive today have ancestors from at least two of the three general racial categories of Negroid, Caucasoid, and Mongoloid (Thompson and Hickey, 2007). With that being said, there probably never were any pure races. Although Montagu (1951) acknowledged three general categories of people, he clearly understood modern humans only exist as one species. In Montagu's words:

> It is clear that there are no "pure races" in existence, and it is greatly to be doubted that there ever were any. The ethnic groups of mankind are not, and never have been, so many separate streams and tributaries flowing within well-defined banks, but currents and eddies in one great river, in which there has been a constant inter-change of what each has carried. (p. 347)

Research supports the view that racial categories should never be viewed as evidence that there are separate species of humans. All modern humans, regardless of race, belong to the species known as *Homo sapiens*. The most recent fossil evidence suggests that the first H. sapiens lived in Morocco, Africa, over 300,000 years ago (Hublin et al., 2017; Kwon, 2017), suggesting that regardless of our race, all of our ancestors migrated from Africa. Furthermore, the mapping of the human genome suggests that the genetic difference between racial categories is actually so small that it is practically insignificant, with racial groups differing only once for every 10,000 genes, or 0.01% (Angler, 2000). Evidence suggests that there is more genetic variability within racial categories than between racial categories

From *Introduction to Sociology* by Jason Hollar and Todd Martin. Copyright © 2018 by Kendall Hunt Publishing Company. Reprinted by permission.

(Witherspoon et al., 2007). In other words, the genetic differences between the "most different" members of a particular race tend to be greater than the average genetic differences between the three races. For example, one study found that there are more genetic differences among Africans from different regions of Africa than there are between Africans and Eurasians (Yu et al., 2002).

A third myth about race is the notion that some races are superior to others. As Henslin (2015) puts it, "All races have their geniuses and their idiots" (p. 254). Nevertheless, throughout history people have acted upon the belief that one race is superior and others are inferior. Examples include (1) the pre–Civil War belief among many plantation owners that black people from Africa are intellectually and morally deficient, are not fully human, need to be controlled, and therefore are fit only to be slaves, and (2) the belief in 1930s Nazi Germany that the Aryan race (Northern European Caucasians) is superior to all others and has a duty to isolate or destroy inferior races that are "lowering the bar" or threatening their birthright as "the leaders of the new world." Tragically, beliefs in racial or ethnic superiority can lead to genocide, as happened in Nazi Germany with the mass murder of Jews and Slavic people, Rwanda in 1994 with the mass murder of ethnic Tutsis by ethnic Hutus, and Bosnia with the mass murder of Muslims by Serbs.

Ethnicity

While race is based on physical characteristics, **ethnicity** refers to a group's distinctive cultural characteristics. Examples of ethnic groups include Jews, Armenians, Gypsies, Tutsis and Hutus (in Rwanda), and Kurds (in parts of Turkey, Iraq, and Iran). Members of ethnic groups tend to have their own language (or at least their own dialect), their own religious beliefs, their own social customs, their own style of dress, their own style of music, and their own style of food. Furthermore, they tend to have a long cultural history in which they identify with each other on the basis of a common ancestry and heritage (Henslin, 2015). In other words, family history is the primary determinant of the ethnic group with which one identifies. As with race, notions of ethnic superiority and inferiority have led to exploitation, slavery, and genocide.

Minority Groups and Dominant Groups

While the standard definition of *minority* for most people is "the group with fewer members," sociologists define this term differently. For sociologists, a **minority group** is a group of people who are singled out, who are treated unequally, and who view themselves as the objects of social discrimination (Wirth, 1945). Using the sociological definition, examples of minority groups include African Americans, women, homosexuals, the elderly, and people with physical handicaps. **Dominant groups**, on the other hand, are the groups with the most power and privileges. It may surprise you to learn that sometimes the minority group is actually larger than the dominant group. For example, during the time of apartheid in South Africa (1948 through the early 1990s), the minority group was the black people and the dominant group was the white people, even though blacks have always far outnumbered whites in this country. There are at least two ways in which a group can become a minority group (Henslin, 2015):

1. Through the expansion of political boundaries (e.g., when the United States took over the southwest in 1848, resulting in the Mexicans who lived there changing from a dominant group into a minority group); and
2. Through migration (e.g., when Africans were brought to the United States to be slaves, sometimes resulting in a status change from a dominant group in Africa into a minority group in the United States).

Reflection Questions: Race, Ethnicity, and Minority Groups

1. Are there just three general racial categories, or are there more? Are the "dark people" of New Guinea and the Outback of Australia and the dark people of Africa both part of the same race (Negroid), or are they different races? Are Native Americans and native Chinese people both part of the same race (Mongoloid), or are they different races? Are dark-haired, tan-skinned Greeks and light-haired, fair-skinned Germans both part of the same race (Caucasoid), or are they different races?
2. What is your opinion regarding the assertion that the genetic differences within races are typically greater than the genetic differences between races (Witherspoon et al., 2007)? What exactly does this assertion mean, and does its truth surprise you?
3. Do you consider yourself a member of a particular ethnic group? If so, which one?
4. Do you consider yourself a member of a particular minority group? If so, which one?

Prejudice and Discrimination

Although these two terms often appear together, prejudice and discrimination are not the same thing. Prejudice is an *attitude*, whereas discrimination is a *behavior*. To be more specific, **prejudice** is an attitude in which a group of people are prejudged in a negative way. Prejudicial beliefs lead to misjudgments because they "ignore the great variation in individual behaviors and focus on a handful of traits that all group members supposedly possess" (Thompson and Hickey, p. 292). For example, a person with prejudice against homosexuals may incorrectly assume that all homosexuals are promiscuous, wildly flamboyant and effeminate (if male), "butch" tomboys (if female), and confrontationally outspoken about their political agenda, whereas in truth, many people with a homosexual orientation do not fit any of these stereotypes. **Discrimination** is unfair treatment directed against an individual because of the group to which he or she belongs. For example, refusing to allow a homosexual student admission into a 4-year college simply because of his sexual orientation is discrimination.

Throughout history, prejudice and discrimination have been directed toward particular races and ethnicities. When these things are directed toward a particular race, we call it **racism**. In the United States, the dominant group has always been Caucasian. Therefore, the objects of racism have tended to be black people (African Americans), "red people" (Native Americans), and "yellow people" (Chinese immigrants in the 19th century and Japanese people during and immediately after World War Two). Sometimes, even well-intended people who make an effort to be open minded make racist assumptions. In his book *Race: How Blacks and Whites Think and Feel about the American Obsession* (Terkel, 1992), author, radio broadcaster, and historian Studs Terkel recounts the following story told to him by an acquaintance:

> My wife was driving down the street in a black neighborhood. The people at the corners were all gesticulating at her. She was very frightened, rolled up the windows, and drove determinedly. She discovered, after several blocks, she was going the wrong way on a one-way street and they were trying to help her. Her assumption was they were blacks and they were out to get her. Mind you, she's a very enlightened person. You'd never associate her with racism, yet her first reaction was that they were dangerous. (p. 3)

In regard to prejudice and discrimination, sociologist Robert Merton (1949) describes four types of people:

1. **All-weather liberals:** People who are neither prejudiced nor discriminate;
2. **Fair-weather liberals:** People who are not prejudiced, but will discriminate if it seems expedient to do so (e.g., a supervisor who has nothing personal against Mexican Americans, but refuses to hire a Mexican American because he is afraid other employees will not approve);

3. **Fair-weather bigots:** People who are prejudiced, but don't discriminate because they fear the consequences (e.g., a supervisor who is prejudiced against Mexican Americans but is willing to hire them because he fears the consequences of breaking the antidiscrimination policies of his company); and
4. **All-weather bigots:** People who are both prejudiced and discriminate (e.g., openly racist members of the Ku Klux Klan).

If you identify as a political conservative, the authors realize that Merton's contrast of the words "liberal" and "bigot" may be offensive to you. Please know that the authors of this textbook do not agree with the implication that all conservatives are bigots. Perhaps Merton's use of the word *liberal* meant "liberated from the bonds of prejudice and discrimination" rather than a reference to a political ideology.

Theories of Prejudice

So why are people prejudiced? This section will describe two psychological theories of prejudice (the scapegoat theory and the authoritarian personality theory) and four sociological theories or perspectives of prejudice (the culture theory, the conflict theory, the functionalist perspective, and the symbolic-interactionist perspective).

Scapegoat Theory

Also known as the *frustration-aggression theory of prejudice*, psychologist John Dollard's **scapegoat theory** (Dollard et al., 1939; Thompson and Hickey, 2007) asserts that when people's desires are blocked, they become angry and frustrated. If they cannot pinpoint the source of their problems or if that source seems too powerful to challenge, frustrated people will identify a scapegoat on which they can vent their anger. These scapegoats are often minorities. An example would be a low-paid white woman working in a textile mill who blames low-paid Mexican American coworkers for her poor salary rather than the people who hired her and set her salary. In her view, "The Mexicans are to blame, because they are willing to work for low wages. The factory would pay me more if they would just go away!" As a result, she gradually becomes more and more prejudiced against Mexican Americans. While venting frustration through prejudice against less-powerful minorities doesn't improve anything, it is a relatively safe way to vent anger and make frustrated people feel superior to somebody (Macionis, 2004).

Authoritarian Personality Theory

Perhaps, a high level of prejudice is related to certain personality types. Psychologist Theodor Adorno's **authoritarian personality theory** (Adorno et al., 1950) asserts that people with authoritarian personalities are more likely to be prejudiced. Authoritarian personalities are people who have a deep respect for authority (Henslin, 2015), rigidly conform to conventional cultural values, see moral issues as clear-cut matters of right and wrong, and see society as competitive with the "better people winning" (Macionis, 2004). Research only partially confirms this theory. While people who are less educated are indeed more likely to be both authoritarian and prejudiced, this doesn't prove that a particular personality type *causes* prejudice. Rather, it simply confirms the long-held understanding that less-educated people tend to be both more authoritarian and more prejudiced (Ray, 1991).

Culture Theory

Also known as the *social distance theory of prejudice*, sociologist Emory Bogardus's **culture theory** (Bogardus, 1968; Macionis, 2004) asserts that everybody is at least somewhat prejudiced because the notion that certain categories of people are inferior is embedded in all cultures. The greater the *social distance,* the more unfavorable attitudes become. For example, in the United States, people tend to feel the "closest" to people with English, Canadian, and Scottish backgrounds, even welcoming intermarriage with these groups. They tend to feel more negative attitudes toward those that they perceive as being the most different from them (e.g., Muslims, Africans, and Asians).

Conflict Theory

The conflict theory of prejudice asserts that powerful people benefit from prejudicial attitudes toward weaker minority groups because the prejudice seems to justify their oppression of many whom they exploit (Macionis, 2004). For example, rich corporate executives can get away with decisions to pay Mexican Americans low wages because many people look down on this group anyway. Also, prejudicial attitudes that drive a wedge between different groups of lower class, working people benefit the powerful elites by discouraging workers from banding together to advance their common interests. The movie *Matewan* illustrates how the hostility between white, African American, and Italian American coal miners in West Virginia in 1920 threatened the solidarity of workers' union attempting to go on strike to force the Stone Mountain Coal Company to provide better conditions to its employees (Rajski, Renzi, and Sayles, 1987).

W.E.B. Du Bois, who was perhaps the most well-known African American sociologist, was a vocal opponent of racism in the early 20th century (Du Bois, 1986; Lewis, 1993, 2000). Du Bois spent years presenting evidence-based arguments that the black race is not inferior to the white race, and is also known as a cofounder of the National Association of Colored Persons (the NAACP). As a proponent of the conflict theory of prejudice, Du Bois (1992) was concerned about the division of workers by race and ethnicity, a phenomenon known as a **split-labor market**. As was the case with striking white coal miners who were replaced with African American and Italian American coal miners in Matewan, West Virginia (Rajski, Renzi, and Sayles, 1987) and with plantation owners in Hawaii when Japanese workers on strike were replaced by Koreans (Jeong and You, 2008), a split labor market allows owners to weaken the bargaining power of workers.

The Functionalist Perspective on Prejudice

Functionalists assert that prejudice against an out-group can strengthen in-group solidarity. Whenever there is a broadly recognized "foreign threat" (e.g., Nazi Germany and Japanese imperialism during World War Two, or Saddam Hussein during the two Iraqi wars), Republican and Democrat congressmen tend to increase their level of cooperation. While nobody really argues that prejudice is a good thing, perhaps it does at least facilitate in-group bonds. Muzafer and Carolyn Sherif found evidence that this may be the case in their Robber's Cave study (Sherif et al., 1961), where two groups of young boys (the Rattlers and the Eagles) were pitted against each other for a series of competitive games at a summer camp. Although the Rattlers and Eagles developed an intense dislike for each other as their competitive rivalry progressed, strong bonds and very little fighting occurred within either of these two groups.

The Symbolic-Interactionist Perspective on Prejudice

Social interactionism asserts that the way in which a society divides races affects how members of that society view reality. Because societies do not all divide up races in the same manner, we do not all see race in the same way. For example, while white Americans perceive Japanese people as being of a different race, to native Nigerians, Japanese and white American people are viewed as being about the same (Thompson and Hickey, 2007). In addition, symbolic interactionism focuses on how *labels* create prejudice (Henslin, 2015). Once labels are applied to a group of people, others tend to exhibit **selective perception**, seeing whatever behavior confirms the label and ignoring whatever does not. For example, if Jewish people are labeled as "money-hungry," others are primed by that label to notice any behavior that seems to confirm it (e.g., Jewish money lenders getting rich off of interest, Jewish merchants overcharging customers) while ignoring any behavior that seems to refute it (e.g., Jews generously supporting charities, as is the case with motion picture director Steven Spielberg [Look to the Stars, 2018]). Even members of the group that has been negatively stereotyped by a label can be affected by this selective perception. For example, a young African American male from the projects who has been labeled a "criminal" or "thug" by others may eventually embrace this label and act accordingly, thinking, "Most of the young black men I see on television, most of the young black rappers I listen to, and most of the young black men in my neighborhood seem to have a 'gangsta thug' image. Maybe I'm destined to be that way too."

Reflection Questions: Theories of Prejudice

1. Between the scapegoat theory, the authoritarian personality theory, the culture theory, and the conflict theory, which theory of prejudice do you think is the truest?
2. Between the scapegoat theory, the authoritarian personality theory, the culture theory, and the conflict theory, are there any theories that you disagree with?
3. What is your opinion of the symbolic-interactionist perspective on prejudice? Does it surprise you that the categorization of races varies somewhat depending on culture (e.g., racial distinctions in the United States vs. Nigeria)? Do you agree with the notion that prejudiced people exhibit selective perception?

Intergroup Relations

Sociologists assert that there are six ways dominant groups and minority groups respond to each other:

1. genocide,
2. population transfer,
3. internal colonialism,
4. segregation,
5. assimilation, and
6. multiculturalism.

The following sections will define and provide examples of each of these six types of intergroup relations.

Genocide

When a dominant group deliberately and systematically tries to eliminate the minority group, we call this act of mass murder **genocide**. Two of the most well-known examples of genocide include the Nazis' attempts to destroy all Jews in German-occupied areas during World War Two, resulting in over 6 million Jewish deaths, and the ethnic Hutus' attempts to destroy all ethnic Tutsis in Rwanda in 1994, resulting in around 800,000 Tutsi deaths (McGreal, 2013). Although most people recoil in horror and disgust at the idea of a genocide and associate it primarily with "the sins of other nations," genocide has also occurred in the United States. For example, the state of California encouraged genocide against Native Americans in the mid-19th century. When gold was discovered in northern California in 1849, about 150,000 Native Americans occupied this area. To get Native Americans "out of the way" in an effort to make room for the incoming whites, the California government put a bounty on their heads, encouraged stealing the horses of dead Native Americans, and reimbursed the bullets of white settlers. In the end, 80% of these California Native Americans (120,000) were dead within 20 years. Although most of these deaths were due to diseases introduced by the new white settlers, quite a few (between 9000 and 16,000) were murdered in cold blood (Blakemore, 2017; Schaefer, 2004).

Population Transfer

The forced transfer of a minority group to a new location is known as **population transfer**. In the United States, the most well-known example of population transfer is the forced relocation of Native Americans to Indian reservations. At the beginning of the 1830s, it is estimated that nearly 125,000 Native Americans lived in the states of Alabama, Florida, Georgia, North Carolina, and Tennessee. Within 10 years, most of them were gone. After the passage of the Indian Removal Act in 1830, the federal government forced most of the Choctaw, Chickasaw, Seminole, Creek, and Cherokee Native Americans living in the southeastern part of the United States to migrate to a specially designated "Indian colonization zone" in Oklahoma to make room for white settlers. The result was a long, difficult, and sometimes dangerous journey called the **Trail of Tears**. Although the law required that this migration be voluntary and free of coercion, President Andrew Jackson often ignored this part of the law by giving tribes the ultimatum to either leave voluntarily or be evicted by the U.S. Army. Most of the Native Americans on the Trail of Tears made the 1000-plus mile journey to Oklahoma on foot, without food, supplies, or any other assistance from the federal government. Many died on the way (History.com Staff, 2009b).

The Trail of Tears is an example of *direct* population transfer. Population transfer can also be *indirect*. For example, the government of czarist Russia never created policies to deliberately expel Russian Jews from the country, but conditions were so bad for Jews living in that country that millions decided to leave voluntarily (Forbes et al., n.d.; Henslin, 2015).

Internal Colonialism

The policy of exploiting minority groups for economic gain is sometimes referred to as **internal colonialism** (Henslin, 2015). Colonialism is a system in which wealthy "mother countries" profit from the labor and natural resources of poor countries under their control. It was prevalent from the 1500s through the 1900s. Even though nearly all former colonies are now independent nations, these countries are sometimes still dependent on their former colonizers, resulting in a situation known as **neocolonialism** (Harrington, 1977).

Internal colonialism differs from traditional colonialism and neocolonialism in that rather than representing a relationship between the people of two different countries, internal colonialism represents a relationship between a minority group and a dominant group *within a single nation*. Otherwise, it is similar to other forms of colonialism. Regardless of type, colonialism allows one group to gain wealth and/or power by exploiting another weaker group under its control. An example of internal colonialism is witnessed in the relationship between the white Afrikaners and the native black people in South Africa during the years of apartheid (1948 through the early 1990s). Wealthy Afrikaner industrial leaders depended on the cheap labor of native South Africans to enhance their profit margins, but in order to do this the black workers had to be "kept in their place" (Burawoy, 1981; Rotich, Ilieva, and Walunywa, 2015).

Segregation

In societies with internal colonialism, minority groups and dominant groups are often segregated (e.g., South Africa during apartheid). **Segregation** can be defined as "the separation of racial or ethnic groups" (Henslin, 2015, p. 270). It is usually imposed by the dominant group to the detriment of the minority group. However, there are also cases where a minority willingly and voluntarily segregates itself from the majority. The Amish people of Ohio and Pennsylvania are an example of voluntary segregation (Macionis, 2004). An obvious example of involuntary, legally enforced segregation is the separation of whites and blacks in the southern part of the United States during the second half of the 19th century and the first half of the 20th century. Jim Crow laws legalized this segregation. Examples of Jim Crow laws were laws requiring movie theaters to provide separate seating for blacks and whites, laws prohibiting white female nurses from being required to tend to African American patients, laws requiring separate seating areas for blacks and whites in restaurants, laws requiring separate public schools for black and white children, and laws prohibiting intermarriage between blacks and whites (Ra, 2016). Typically, segregation was *not* equal, with whites benefiting from better service in hospitals and restaurants, better funded and equipped schools, etc.

Assimilation

In other societies, minority groups are absorbed into the mainstream. Eventually, they lose their distinctive identities and adopt the cultural traditions of the dominant group. This process is known as **assimilation**. Typically, this is a slow process in which the minority group gradually adopts the style of dress, values, religion, and language of the dominant groups (maybe over a few generations). Advantages of assimilation are that the ability to blend in can lead to greater social mobility and fewer experiences of discrimination and prejudice (Macionis, 2004). However, the primary disadvantage of assimilation is that old traditions passed down over many generations can be lost, along with the sense of belonging and camaraderie that often comes with identifying with a particular ethnicity. Examples of ethnic groups that have gradually assimilated into American culture include German, Irish, and Japanese Americans. Sometimes, assimilation is forced rather than voluntary. An example of forced assimilation is the imperial Japanese policy toward Korea when it was a Japanese colony (1910–1945). The Japanese colonizers forbade the usage of the Korean language in schools and required Koreans to worship at shrines to the native religion of Japan, Shinto (Blakemore, 2018; Ho and Park, 2004; Michio, 2010).

Multiculturalism

Also known as *pluralism,* **multiculturalism** occurs when racial and ethnic groups have achieved equality while still retaining their distinct cultural identities. In multicultural societies, even though groups are distinct and different, there is a fairly high degree of **social parity**, meaning the different groups share resources more or less equally, and are viewed as equal in the eyes of the law (Macionis, 2004). Large cities in the United States are excellent examples of multiculturalism. Canada enacted multiculturalism as a federal policy over 50 years ago, enshrining this in its Multiculturalism Act. Elsewhere, multiculturalism can be witnessed at smaller scales. For example, New York City has a variety of ethnic neighborhoods, including Spanish Harlem, Little Italy, and Chinatown. Although Little Italy, once home to thousands of Italian Americans, has shrunk to about three blocks and is perhaps less authentic (i.e., more "touristy") than the other two neighborhoods (Harris, 2018), ethnic foods are still easy to find in all three neighborhoods. Furthermore, although English is now the dominant language in Spanish Harlem (especially among the younger generation), Spanish is still common there (Shousterman, 2014), and Chinese dialects such as Mandarin and Cantonese dominate in Chinatown (Semple, 2009). Chinatown in particular has the feel of a foreign country, with most storefront signs advertising in Chinese (or other Asian scripts such as Korean, Japanese, or Hindi) rather than English (Bilefsky, 2011). Nevertheless, all three of these ethnic groups in New York City have equal standing under the law.

Reflection Questions: Intergroup Relations

1. Consider the Rwandan genocide. What conditions make it possible for neighbors to kill neighbors or friends to kill friends, as was often the case with the Hutu genocide against the Tutsis? How might the Rwandan genocide have been prevented?
2. Do you believe racial or ethnic hatred can spread like a disease, causing people to lose their capacity for compassion, reason, and independent thought? Can nice people be induced by "mob groupthink" to commit violent acts, or were these simply evil people to begin with?
3. Compare assimilation to multiculturalism. In the long run, do you believe it is better for ethnic groups to give up old languages and customs in order to fit in better with the dominate group, or is it better for ethnic groups to hang on to their languages and customs in order to preserve their ethnic identities?

References

Adorno, T. W., E. Frenkel-Brunswick, D. J. Levinson, and R, N. Sanford. 1950. *The Authoritarian Personality.* New York, NY: Harper & Row.

Angler, N. August 22, 2000. Do Races Differ? Not Really, DNA Shows. *New York Times.* http://www.nytimes.com/2000/08/22/science/do-races-differ-not-really-genes-show.html

Bilefsky, D. August 1, 2011. In Neighborhood That's Diverse, a Push for Signs to Be Less So. *The New York Times.* https://www.nytimes.com/2011/08/02/nyregion/queens-councilman-wants-english-to-dominate-store-signs.html

Blakemore, E. November 16, 2017. California's Little Known Genocide. *History.com.* https://www.history.com/news/californias-little-known-genocide

B Blakemore, E. February 27, 2018. How Japan Took Control of Korea. *History.com.* https://www.history.com/news/japan-colonization-korea

ogardus, E. 1968. "Comparing Racial Distance in Ethiopia, South Africa, and the United States." *Sociology and Social Research* 52 (2): 149–56.

Burawoy, M. 1981. "The Capitalist State in South Africa: Marxist and Sociological Perspectives on Race and Class." *Political Power and Social Theory* 2: 279–335.

Dollard, J., L. W. Doob, N. E. Miller, O. H. Mowrer, and R. R. Sears. 1939. *Frustration and Aggression.* New Haven, CT: Yale University Press.

Du Bois, W. E. B. 1986. The souls of Black folk. In *W.E.B. Du Bois: Writings.* Edited by N. Huggins, 357–547. New York, NY: Library of America.

Du Bois, W. E. B. 1992. *Black Reconstruction in America: An Essay Toward a History of the Part Which Black Folk Played in the Attempt to Reconstruct Democracy in America, 1860-1880.* New York, NY: Atheneum.

Forbes, E., S. Lauer, K. Koonz, and P. Sweeney. n.d. A Resource Guide for Teachers: Russian Jewish Immigration 1880-1920. Fitchburg State University. http://www.fitchburgstate.edu/uploads/files/TeachingAmericanHistory/RussianJews.pdf

Harrington, M. 1977. *The Vast Majority: A Journey to the World's Poor.* New York, NY: Simon & Schuster.

Harris, E. A. February 19, 2018. Little Italy Is Very Little, and Not Very Italian. *The New York Times.* https://www.nytimes.com/2018/02/19/nyregion/little-italy-manhattan-fire.html

Henslin, J. M. 2015. *Essentials of Sociology: A Down-to-Earth Approach.* 11th edition. Upper Saddle River, NJ: Pearson.

Ho, K., and J. Park. 2004. Manifestations of Ethnic Prejudices Derived from the Japanese Occupation of Korea and Taiwan: The Asian Experience vs. the Asian-American Experience. *EDGE*. http://web.stanford.edu/class/e297a/Japanese%20Occupation%20of%20Korea%20and%20Taiwan%20-%20The%20Asian%20vs%20The%20Asian-%20American%20Experiencea.doc.

Hublin, J.-J., A. Ben-Ncer, S. E. Bailey, S. E. Freidline, S. Neubauer, M. M. Skinner, I. Bergmann, A. Le Cabec, S. Benazzi, K. Harvati, and P. Gunz. 2017. "New Fossils from Jebel, Morocco and the Pan-African Origin of Homo Sapiens." *Nature* 546: 289–92.

Jeong, Y.-J.,and H. -K. You. 2008. "Different Historical Trajectories and Family Diversity Among Chinese, Japanese, and Koreans in the United States." *Journal of Family History* 33 (3): 346–56.

Justia Legal Resources. 2018. Brown v. Board of Education of Topeka, 347 U.S. 483 (1954). *Justia U.S. Supreme Court.* https://supreme.justia.com/cases/federal/us/347/483/case.html

Kwon, D. June 7, 2017. Scientists Uncover Oldest Homo Sapiens Fossils to Date. *The Scientist*. https://www.the-scientist.com/?articles.view/articleNo/49623/title/Scientists-Uncover-Oldest-Homo-sapiens-Fossils-to-Date/

Lewis, D. L. 1993. *W.E.B. Du Bois: A Biography of Race 1868-1919*. New York, NY: Henry Holt and Company.

Lewis, D. L. 2000. *W.E.B. Du Bois: The Fight for Equality and the American Century 1919-1963*. New York, NY: Henry Holt and Company. https://books.google.com/books?id=RD75BE1Alr4C&printsec=frontcover&dq=d.l.+lewis+(2001).+W.E.B.+Du+Bois+The+fight+for+equality&hl=en&sa=X&ved=0ahUKEwiDl8qFhIHaAhUBy1MKHYN5C9sQ6AEIKTAA#v=onepage&q&f=false

Look to the Stars. 2018. Steven Spielberg: Charity Work, Events, and Causes. *Look to the Stars: The World of Celebrity Giving.* https://www.looktothestars.org/celebrity/steven-spielberg

Macionis, J. J. 2004. *Sociology.* 10th edition. Upper Saddle River, NJ: Prentice Hall.

McGreal, C. May 12, 2013. Rwanda Genocide 20 Years on: "We Live with Those Who Killed Our Families. We Are Told They Are Sorry, But Are They?" *The Guardian.* https://www.theguardian.com/world/2013/may/12/rwanda-genocide-20-years-on

Merton, R. K. 1949. Discrimination and the American creed. In *Discrimination and National Welfare*. Edited by R. M. MacIver, 99–126. New York, NY: Institute for Religious Studies.

Michio, N. (2010). "Shinto Deities that Crossed the sea: Japanese Overseas Shrines, 1868-1945." *Japanese Journal of Religious Studies* 37 (1): 21–46.

Montagu, M. F. A. 1942. *Man's Most Dangerous Myth: The Fallacy of Race.* New York, NY: Columbia University Press.

Montagu, M. F. A. 1951. *An Introduction to Physical Anthropology.* 2nd edition. Springfield, IL: Charles C. Thomas Publisher. https://archive.org/stream/introductiontoph033240mbp/introductiontoph033240mbp_djvu.txt

Montagu, M. F. A. 1964. *The Concept of Race.* New York, NY: Free Press.

Ra, F. October 8, 2016. 17 Examples of Jim Crow Laws in the United States of America. *Urban Intellectuals.* https://urbanintellectuals.com/2016/10/08/17-examples-of-jim-crow-laws-in-the-united-states-of-america/

Rajski, P., M., and J. Sayles, J. 1987. *Matewan* [Motion Picture]. United States: Cinecom Pictures.

Ray, J. J. 1991. "Authoritarianism Is a Dodo: Comment on Scheepers, Felling and Peters." *European Sociological Review* 7 (1): 73–5.

Rotich, R., E. V. Ilieva, and J. Walunywa. 2015. "The Social Formation of Post-apartheid South Africa." *The Journal of Pan African Studies* 8 (9): 132–55. www.jpanafrican.org/docs/vol8no9/8.9-11-RRotich.pdf

Schaefer, R. T. 2004. *Racial and Ethnic Groups.* 9th edition. Upper Saddle River, NJ: Prentice Hall.

Semple, K. October 21, 2009. In Chinatown, Sound of the Future is Mandarin. *The New York Times.* https://www.nytimes.com/2009/10/22/nyregion/22chinese.html

Sherif, M., O. J. Harvey, B. J. White, W. R., and C. W. Sherif. 1961. *Intergroup Conflict and Cooperation: The Robbers Cave Experiment.* Vol. 10. Norman, OK: University Book Exchange.

Shousterman, K. 2014. "Speaking English in Spanish Harlem: The role of Rhythm." *University of Pennsylvania Working Papers in Linguistics* 20 (2): 18. https://repository.upenn.edu/cgi/viewcontent.cgi?article=1823&context=pwpl

Terkel, S. 1992. *Race: How Blacks and Whites Think and Feel about the American Obsession.* New York, NY: New Press.

Thompson, W. E., and J. V. Hickey. 2007. *Society in Focus: An Introduction to Sociology.* 6th edition. Boston, MA: Allyn & Bacon.

Wirth, L. 1945. The problem of minority groups. In *The Science of Man in the World Crisis.* Edited by Ralph Linton, 347–72. New York, NY: Columbia University Press.

Witherspoon, D. J., S. Wooding, A. R. Rogers, E. E. Marchani, W. S. Watkins, M. A. Batzer, and L. B. Jorde. 2007. *Genetics* 176 (1): 351–9.

Yu, N., F. -C. Chin, S. Ota, L. B. Jorde, P. Pamilo, L. Patthy, M. Ramsay, T. Jenkins, S. -K. Shyue, and W.- S. Li. 2002. "Larger Genetic Differences within Africans than Between Africans and Eurasians." *Genetics* 161 (1): 269–74.

9 Social Change and Social Movements

Learning Objectives

9.1 Understand sociological theories pertaining to social change and social movements

9.2 Identify various types of social movements

9.3 Examine motivations for social change and social movements

Perspectives on Social Change

There's a saying that goes, "change is the only constant"; for social phenomena, this couldn't hold more true. Social change and social movements are best looked at as results of changing norms in society. They can also be looked at as individuals joining together and mobilizing as a unit to create change within a society. In order to start examining what social movements and social change are, we first need to understand how classic perspectives view social change and its role within society.

© mindscanner/Shutterstock.com

Functionalist Perspective

Functionalists assume that society is ever-evolving and will continue to change because the composition of societies will continue to change. As we have discussed thus far in this text, over the course of multiple generations, major institutions such as the family, education, and so on, have all changed. The purpose may remain the same, but the processes of those institutions have evolved and that is because society itself has evolved. Functionalists believe that as societies continue to develop, they do so by becoming more complex and interdependent. This concept follows along Durkheim's notion of the division of labor which examines the differentiation of people into various categories, social roles, and institutions. Furthering this, when we review the concepts of organic solidarity and mechanical solidarity, we come to realize that as society further evolves into interdisciplinary parts, so too do groups of people. To better conceptualize this, think back to

Organic Solidarity: This is social unity based on a division of labor that results in people depending on each other.

the time when the American society was characterized as agrarian. A farmer has to buy feed from a supplier for his cattle, as the cattle matures, he then sells it to a butcher, and the butcher then sells the meat. This is a small segment of society, but displays how these three people are interdependent upon one another. In modern society, we could successfully argue that our lives have become even more interdependent.

Mechanical Solidarity: This is the sense of togetherness in a society that arises when people, performing similar work, share similar experiences, customs, values, and beliefs.

Earlier functionalist theories concentrated on this concept of evolution, and focused on the basic principles that earlier societies were primitive and over time would develop into more complex, distinguished societies (Morgan 1877/1964). These evolutionist theories moved from being unilinear in the nineteenth century to multilinear in the twentieth century by claiming that it was too simplistic and myopic to believe that all societies evolved in the same way toward the same goals. During this time, practitioners recognized that social change is predicated on a multitude of variables and presents itself differently for each situation in society (Moore 2004; Sahlins and Service 1960).

Conflict Perspective

For conflict theorists, social movements and social change are the result of conflict in society and therefore, they are a result of society demanding change—usually for the equalization within a specific phenomenon. While functionalists view social change as natural growing pains for a society, conflict theorists see social change as the final breakdown of society unequally distributing power and individuals being subjected to oppression and marginalization. For Marx, he hoped that societies would come to realize that there is unequal distribution of power and wealth; and therefore, would engage in social change and movements as a means to move toward a classless society. In addition to Marx's ideas, Italian theorist Gramsci (1971) claimed that the ruling class created a society in which they continuously oppressed the lower classes. Furthering this, Dahrendorf (1958) claimed that social change was necessary as it highlighted the oppression of people and to argue otherwise would indicate that oppression in society was acceptable. We see the combination of these two theorists' point of view when we examine such social movements as the social rights movements in the 1960s and the women's movement in the 1970s. Both movements challenged the status quo which previously indicated that it was acceptable to oppress people based on race and gender.

Rise-and-Fall Theories

Rise-and-fall theories examine social change and movements as naturally occurring growth patterns in society. These theories differ from the ideas held by functionalists in that rise-and-fall theories hold a

Rise-and-Fall Theories: Theories which claim social growth is cyclical.

biblical or life-cycle approach rather than understanding social change as simply that, change. In understanding these theories, we draw our attention to Sorokin (1957/1970, 1962) who was a historical sociologist and claimed that societies are essentially comprised of three different rationalities. These rationalities mirror the three stages of growth as first introduced by Comte: societies which follow their senses, societies which emphasize religiosity, and societies that emphasize logic and reason. These can be viewed as states of growth for industrialized societies or serve as categories in which to group societies in.

Social Change: Where Does It Come From

When we see social change and social movements occur, we need to stop and analyze where they came from. Often, what we see is the result of individuals mobilizing themselves and challenging social norms and the breakdown of institutional structure. When we think of social movements, we can probably name one or two key individuals who are associated with those movements. For example, when we look at the suffragette movement, you probably think of the names Elizabeth Cady Stanton and Lucretia Mott. But, they were two of thousands of women who banded together to impart change in society. In this section, we are going to look at different ways that people mobilize.

Collective Behavior

Collective behavior describes individuals voluntarily coming together in usually disorganized events. There are various forms of collective behavior and theories which help to understand how people come together in response to changing norms in society. Crowds are something that we are familiar with, perhaps you can recall a time in which you were in a crowd. Crowds are a temporary gathering of people usually with an intended focus. An example of a crowd might be individuals waiting in line to get into the mall early for Thanksgiving Day shopping. Usually, crowds represent some aspect of apprehension for individuals because they can develop quickly a herd mentality and emotions may run high in a crowded situation. Blumer (1951) examined this herd mentality by drawing on the interactionist perspective and stated that when people are grouped together, such as in a crowd, then they tend to imitate behavior—this

Collective Behavior: It refers to events that suddenly emerge.

Crowds: A large number of people gathered together, typically in a disorganized or unruly way.

phenomenon is the focus point of contagion theories. Contagion theories are theories which examine group behavior that becomes contagious. Have you ever been to a concert and just got swept up in what the crowd was doing, or perhaps similarly at a sporting event? These are examples of how crowd behavior can alter individual behavior due to their contagious nature.

Contagion Theories: They propose that crowds exert a hypnotic influence on their members.

Emergent norm theories allow us to examine crowd behavior in terms of understanding norms that are created from such behavior. Externally, the crowd may be chaotic, but internally there are norms that are governing the crowd's behavior. An example of this would be the Tea Party movement which called for a Republican party and lessening of government spending and debt reduction. Emergent norm theories allow us to understand how crowds are established and maintained. They indicate that crowds tend to emerge from a common set of norms, rather than recreating or establishing new norms. They tend to illustrate that crowds are often formed spontaneously, rather than being a planned event; and the norms associated with crowds do not fully inform us of the collective behavior that is displayed. Value-added theory helps us to understand the larger, or macro, perspective of crowd behavior such as poverty, institutional faults, abuse of power, and much more. Now that we have a theoretical framework for understanding crowds, we will examine how they work and how they present themselves in various forms..

Emergent Norm Theory: This states that crowd behavior is guided by unique social norms, which are established by members of the crowd.

Value-Added Theory: This is based on the assumption that certain conditions are needed for the development of a social movement.

Riots

Riots are classified as illegal and usually violent behavior. They tend to be spontaneous and their destructive behavior can be targeted at individuals or property. Historically, the Boston Tea Party can be categorized as a riot; and more recently, the riots which occurred in the 1960s in Newark, Los Angeles, and Detroit.

Riots: A violent disturbance of the peace by a crowd.

Fads and Fashions

Fads are classified as temporary, highly imitated behavior. A popular fad that is currently taking place is using the phrase, "Keep Calm and _____" or shaving one side of your head. Fashion, on the other hand while highly imitated tends to last longer than a fad. It was fashionable to listen to grunge music or shop from the catalog Delia's in the 1990s. Currently,

Fads: An intense and widely shared enthusiasm for something, especially one that is short-lived and without basis in the object's qualities.

Fashion: A popular trend, especially in styles of dress and ornament or manners of behavior.

it's fashionable to use hashtags in social media for various reasons.

Panics and Crazes

When someone is in a state of panic, they are seeking refuge from something they fear. This behavior might lead people to think or act irrationally. For example, in 1999, many people were panicking because they assumed that when it became the year 2000 that the computer systems would shut down. As a result, people started buying gold, making bunkers, and not trusting major institutions. Crazes are classified as an intense attraction to someone or something. When the Twilight series came out, it had a huge following which earned its fans the name of Twihards.

Panic: Sudden uncontrollable fear or anxiety, often causing wildly unthinking behavior.

Craze: An enthusiasm for a particular activity or object that typically appears suddenly and achieves widespread but short-lived popularity.

Rumors

Rumors are informal pieces of information that often reflect the insecurities of the person passing along the information. Rumors can only be effective if they are able to speak to a wide-held fear by the public or person of interest.

Social Movements

Social movements are classified as large numbers of people who come together in an organized effort to create change. We have already touched upon some popular social movements that you have learned about in this book or perhaps your history classes. Currently, there is a social movement advocating for the government to change its stance on the ownership of firearms. This movement has come about because of the multitude of school shootings that we have seen in recent years. Not all social movements are created for the same purpose. We will now take a look at various social movements.

Rumor: A currently circulating story or report of uncertain or doubtful truth.

Social Movements: They are large, sometimes informal, groupings of individuals, or organizations which focus on specific political or social issues.

Reformist Movements

Reformist movements are created to bring social change to current economic and social institutions. Typically, these type of movements exist in democratic societies. The suffrage movement, civil rights movement, and the labor movement are excellent examples of reformist movements.

> **Reformist Movements:** A type of social movement that aims to make gradual change, or change in certain aspects of society, rather than rapid or fundamental changes.

Revolutionary Movements

Revolutionary movements are movements which seek to completely get rid of previous economic and social institutions and make new ones in their place. These movements exist because there is a strong presence of oppression, so much so that a reformist movement would not create any change. Revolutionary movements tend to focus on government issues; the American Revolution, Arab Spring, and the Apartheid movement in South Africa are excellent examples of revolutionary movements.

> **Revolutionary Movements:** They are a specific type of social movement dedicated to carrying out a revolution.

Rebellions

Rebellions are movements that seek to overthrow the current social, economic, and political system. Rebellions exist in situations where it is difficult to formally organize. A famous example is the Nat Turner rebellion in the 1800s, or the Louis Riel and Metis rebellion in Canada in the same period.

Reactionary Movements

Reactionary movements are created when the goal is to restore previous social systems. Often, these movements are a reaction to changing norms. The Ku Klux Klan and the White Aryan Resistance are examples of reactionary movements.

> **Rebellions:** An act of violent or open resistance to an established government or ruler.

> **Reactionary Movements:** They advocate the restoration of a previous state of social affairs, while a progressive movement argues for a new social arrangement.

Conclusion

Social change and social movements are the ebbs and flow of society growing and changing. As a society progresses, it must constantly engage dialogically with norms and values within the society. Social movements offer opportunity for people to challenge the status quo, they equalize areas of society that have created a sense of marginality. Currently, we are seeing people mobilize to secure a safer learning environment for school-aged children. This is not a conversation about the right to bear arms; but rather a multitude of conversations which encompass concepts of privilege, status, safety, and infrastructure. As we progress and change, so too will the ways in which mobilize. Today, not only do we physically march, but we electronically march by using the hashtag and posting events which call us to gather, on social media. The stage for change might be evolving; but the need for people to gather in the collective will always remain the same.

Activity

Go to http://www.minyanville.com/businessmarkets/articles/10-movements-that-changed-america-movements/11/4/2011/id/37721 and examine the popular social movements. Pick a social movement from the site and a current social movement and critically analyze their similarities and differences.

_____
_____
_____
_____
_____
_____
_____
_____
_____
_____
_____
_____
_____
_____
_____
_____
_____
_____
_____
_____

10 The State

Learning Objectives

10.1 Examine concepts of the state, power, and terrorism

10.2 Apply sociological perspectives in examining the state

10.3 Understand concepts of political systems

The State

Many of us watch the news today, and we're familiar with concepts such as **state**, **nation**, and what they are made of. When sociologists examine the concepts of state we're looking at groups of people that are united by bodies of government, that have been formed through the creation of boundaries, sometimes through the creation of war, and various other ways that nations are created. The state is key in understanding the society around us because the state is essentially what a group of people is, it helps us to understand our identity, and it also helps us to understand our rights, privileges, and our connection to something greater. In sociology, we also examine not only the state in which we live, but also how the nation or the states that we live in then interact(s) with other nations and states around the world. Global conversations encompass many things such as healthcare, religion, education, and a plethora of other social situations.

State: A nation or territory considered as an organized political community under one government.

Nation: A large aggregate of people united by common descent, history, culture, or language, inhabiting a particular country or territory.

One of the concepts that we will examine within this chapter is the notion of citizenship. We have heard the word citizenship and the phrase **citizens'** rights both in various classes throughout the years and, also, in our media and social media. It is important to understand the current conversations which define what it means to be a citizen and the rights that are attributed. Many of the conversations regarding the process of becoming a citizen, particularly in the United States, concentrate on the global impact regarding the relationship between the United States and other countries. Citizens of any given country are eligible for rights within that country; these rights include access to public education, healthcare, the opportunity to vote, and many other rights that we as a society often take for granted. What are some of the rights that you consider eligible to individuals who are citizens? **Citizenship rights** are juxtaposed to social rights which actually call for government help or assistance. Similar social rights that we examine in the discipline of sociology are economic rights such as social security or healthcare such as Medicare and Medicaid. These programs often are scrutinized because of the parameters that are encompassed within the rights themselves. For many individuals, particularly the working poor, it is really difficult to fully utilize some of the social rights that the nation can offer. However in contemporary conversation, such as what you will see in the news, over the past several years, there has been more and more pressure placed upon legislators to create even stronger parameters in order to ensure that people are not abusing the system. Additionally, **social rights** are a benchmark to illustrate how economically advanced a nation our country is. Essentially, the more economically advanced nations or states have more social programs that allow the government to help provide assistance for its citizens.

Citizens: A legally recognized subject or national of a state or commonwealth, either native or naturalized.

Citizenship Rights: The rights belonging to an individual by virtue of citizenship.

Social Rights: Economic, social, and cultural rights are socioeconomic human rights, such as the right to education, right to housing, right to adequate standard of living, right to health, and the right to science and culture.

Theories of the State

Functionalist Perspective

Per many of the discussions that we have had in this textbook, we're going to draw upon the teachings of Emile Durkheim. Practitioners who examine social phenomenon via the functionalist perspective asked the question, "how does this institution provide a function?" As for Durkheim, he saw the government as an institution that was supposed to be neutral and provide a platform in which citizens of the state could bring forth any issues to the government and the government would be able to handle it in a very neutral manner. With this concept, Durkheim was assuming that the government was going to be a neutral body and that the nation was going to have the same comprehension of norms and values within the society.

Conflict Perspective and Class Dominance Theory

Naturally, when we examine issues of conflict or an equal distribution of resources including class, we're going to first draw on Karl Marx. With this theoretical paradigm, we understand that nations and societies are not equal; they are comprised of varying classes, resources, and distribution of power. Therefore, when we examine the nation or state utilizing the conflict perspective, we are examining how power is distributed throughout the society and how this inevitably leads to social conflict. When we study core Marxist teachings, we understand that the government is seen as an elite organization. It is comprised of individuals who have access to power, resources, money, and have the ability to rule, whereas the citizens of the nation are likened to that of the lower classes and therefore lack what the government possesses. We examine the conflict perspective in contemporary society, we examine what is known as **class dominance theory**. This theory claims that power is concentrated in the hands of the very few. Some of the questions that we ask when examining class dominance theory are "who benefits" and "who wins" Many of these questions should draw your attention to some of the stories that you may have perhaps

Karl Marx.

seen in the social media or while watching a news program; some of these questions will also help you to understand concepts around lobbyists, around general elections, and other forms of governance.

Class Dominance Theory: Small, concentrated group of elite or upper-class individuals dominate and influence social institutions.

Types of Power and Authority

Traditional Authority

The types of authority that social practitioners understand are the ones that are presented to us by Weber (1921/1979). When we examine the state, and politics in general, we tend to think of varying kinds of authority. One type of authority is traditional authority. Traditional authority is exactly what it sounds like, it is set in tradition. It is a form of authority in which the power is vested in the sanctity of the individual and that individual has done nothing to prove that they are worthy of the authority. A common example of this type of authority is the Queen of England.

Many nations that use traditional authority also coexist with rational-legal authority. Traditional authority, in this instance, exhibits that it operates at various levels.

Traditional Authority: A form of leadership in which the authority of an organization or a ruling regime is largely tied to tradition or custom.

Rational-Legal Authority

Rational-legal authority is the type of authority that is founded in an understanding of the law. Individuals who are considered to have rational-legal authority are done so by the belief that they will uphold a lawfulness for the nation, or community. Examples of rational-legal authority are individuals that are voted into various offices such as president, Prime Minister, or member of parliament. In this system, individuals only hold authority as long as they continue to be lawful. When an individual acts in a way that is unlawful, then they will no longer hold authority. An example of this is when president Bill Clinton cheated on his wife, and first lady, Hillary Clinton with Monica Lewinski. The people of the United States regarded him as president, until the scandal

Rational-Legal Authority: A form of leadership in which the authority of an organization or a ruling regime is largely tied to legal rationality, legal legitimacy, and bureaucracy.

emerged, then his authority was diminished for some people. As president of the United States, he symbolically represents the norms and values of the community, one being marital faithfulness; when he indicated that he couldn't be faithful to his wife, then many of his constituents wondered if he would be faithful to them as their president.

Charismatic Authority

We have all met someone in our life that seems to have a presence about them; they have a personality that draws you in. This type of individual would be considered charismatic. Some individuals who have been given authority have received that position simply based on their charismatic personality. Charismatic authority is the type of authority that is bestowed to someone based on the devotion of the followers. They do not have authority that has been passed down from generations, as is the case with traditional authority; and they do not possess authority because they legally uphold rules, as with rational-legal authority. Charismatic leaders are often stigmatized as being malevolent in society, but many positive changes have come about in society because of these types of leaders.

Charismatic Authority: Power based on devotion by the personal qualities of a leader rather than legal qualifications.

Types of Government

As we have just seen, there are different types of authority found within many communities around the world. Additionally, there are different types of government as well.

Totalitarianism: A system of government that is centralized and dictatorial and requires complete subservience to the state.

Totalitarianism

A totalitarian government is one in which the governing body denies political participation from its constituents and regulates control over both the public and private spheres of citizens' lives. An example you may be familiar with from your history classes is the Soviet leader Vladimir Lenin, or even Adolf Hitler. They were leaders that controlled every aspect of their citizens' lives and even went one step further in that they ruled through the use of fear. Practitioners examine these types of communities and try to understand how citizens are not able to retain control, express freedom or agency, and how this impacts other institutions.

Authoritarianism

Authoritarianism is a type of governance in which citizens are not allowed to participate in the government and the political power is exercised through a small body of elite individuals. Examples of this type of government are absolute monarchies and dictatorships. Authoritarianism is not as common around the world as it used to be, one reason being that it is simply too difficult and impractical for one family or small group to rule an entire country or nation. Regarding the monarchy, the Queen or King is still head of the church and state, but much of the decision-making and policy formation come from specialized departments within the government system—not from the Royal family.

Authoritarianism: The enforcement or advocacy of strict obedience to authority at the expense of personal freedom.

Democracy

A **democracy** is a form of government that is ruled by the people. It is the form of government used in places such as the European Union, Canada, Australia, Japan and many others. In a democratic system, the citizens choose their representatives—known as **representative democracy**. In a democracy, the citizens have the right to choose who is voted into office and to voice their concerns about issues that they see happening in their nation.

Democracy: A system of government by the whole population or all the eligible members of a state, typically through elected representatives.

Representative Democracy: A type of democracy founded on the principle of elected officials representing a group of people.

Terrorism

In today's society, terrorism is unfortunately a common word. Since the 2011 attacks on the Twin Towers in New York City and other major events in France, Belgium and England, we have been on a hypervigilant alert for any person or situation that may be conclude in a terrorist attack. Unfortunately, in many aspects, this fear has altered how many people live their lives and how they treat individuals. Since 2011, Islamophobia has increased and many programs, both academically and socially, have been created to counter hate crimes which have stemmed from the sentiment of recent terrorist attacks. When you think of a terrorist, who comes to mind? A terrorist is any individual who inflicts fear or terror on individuals. There is no set race, ethnicity, class, national affiliation, or educational obtainment level that will determine if an individual will be a terrorist. Terrorism is any act that creates fear; it can be local or global. Recently, there has been an increase in school shootings in the United States. The people that have been involved in these shootings are technically terrorists; why do we not call them as such? Many practitioners in the United States of America believe that since the creation of the War on Terrorism, in response to the September 11 attacks, we have conceptualized a terrorist or terrorism as an act of "other"—it is someone else, not our neighbor, not our friend, someone over there; and it is something that another nation inflicts upon us, rather than it happening within our national limits. If we examine how we have conversations about nations and terrorism, we must examine them through a multitude of lenses, one being how we symbolically label the individuals creating these situations, and where the situations are taking place.

Terrorist: A person who uses unlawful violence and intimidation, especially against civilians, in the pursuit of political aims.

Terrorism: Unlawfully using violence and intimidation, especially against civilians, in the pursuit of political aims.

Conclusion

When examining concepts of the state, it is important to understand that they are continuously evolving as are the institutions that they serve and interact with. Many of us imagined when we were younger what it would be like to be president; perhaps you have experience being the president of your class or club. Being in a position of authority is a very difficult job because there are many global and local issues that are constantly changing. As practitioners, it is imperative that we examine how nations and states interact with one another on a global stage, and how each nation is both independent and interdependent of the other nations it shares that stage with.

Activity

Pick a news story from either a local newspaper or national website and examine it sociologically. Identify what are the concepts of power that the article is discussing, what are some of the issues it is addressing, is this a new problem, or one that is continuously present?

CPSIA information can be obtained
at www.ICGtesting.com
Printed in the USA
BVHW022343070123
655774BV00002B/5